I0091873

The Roman Cemetery at Gerulata Rusovce, Czechoslovakia

Ľudmila Kraskovská

revised by the author

translated from the Slovak by
Hana Schuck

BAR Supplementary Series 10
1976

British Archaeological Reports

122 Banbury Road, Oxford OX2 7BP, England

GENERAL EDITORS

A.C.C. Brodribb, M.A.
Mrs. Y.M. Hands

A.R. Hands, B.Sc., M.A.,
D.Phil. D.R. Walker, B.A.

B.A.R. Supplementary Series 10, 1976: "The Roman Cemetery at Gerulata Rusovce, Czechoslovakia"

© Ľudmila Kraskovská, Slovenské Národné Múzeum, Bratislava, Czechoslovakia

The author's moral rights under the 1988 UK Copyright,
Designs and Patents Act are hereby expressly asserted.

All rights reserved. No part of this work may be copied, reproduced, stored,
sold, distributed, scanned, saved in any form of digital format or transmitted
in any form digitally, without the written permission of the Publisher.

ISBN 9780904531428 paperback
ISBN 9781407324968 e-book
DOI https://doi.org/10.30861/9780904531428
A catalogue record for this book is available from the British Library
This book is available at www.barpublishing.com

CONTENTS

LIST OF ILLUSTRATIONS

Page

Please note that additional material is available to download from
www.barpublishing.com/additional-downloads.html.
The original foldout has been reduced in size to match the A4 format of this book, the
image is therefore not as clear as the original foldout. Please refer to the original
foldout via the download for the original content.

ABBREVIATIONS

AAH	Acta Archaeologica Akademiae Scientiarum Hungaricae, Budapest
AÉ	Archeologiai értesitő, Budapest
AR	Archeologické rozhledy, Praha
AReg	Alba Regia, Székesfehérvár
Ber RGK	Bericht der Römisch-Germanischen Kommission, Frankfurt a. M.
BJ	Bonner Jahrbücher, Bonn
BR	Budapest régiségei, Budapest
DP	Dissertationes Pannonicae, Budapest
FA	Folia Archaeologica, Budapest
Intercisa I	Barkóczi, L., et al.: Intercisa I. (Dunapentele-Sztálinváros). Geschichte der Stadt in der Römerzeit. Budapest 1954.
Intercisa II	Alföldi, M., et al.: Intercisa II. (Dunapentele). Geschichte der Stadt in der Römerzeit, Budapest 1957
PA	Památky archeologické, Praha
SbNM	Sborník Národního muzea, Praha
SlA	Slovenská archeológia, Nitra
SMSS	Sbornik Muzealnej slovenskej spolocnosti, Martin
ŠZ AÚSAV	Študijné zvesti Archeologického ústavu Slovenskej akadémie vied, Nitra
ZbSNM	Zborník Slovenského národného múzea, Bratislava

Frontispiece: Glass jug, Grave 1

INTRODUCTION

Rusovce parish, in Bratislava-vidiek district, is situated on the right bank of the Danube 13 km from Bratislava (Map, fig. 1). Over many years of archaeological research in the parish very rich finds have been made of material dating back to the Roman settlement at Bergl and also from a few Roman burials in this parish. The results of this research show an extensive Roman settlement at Rusovce dating from the end of the 1st to the end of the 4th century A.D. The evidence enables us to date Roman Gerulata in the parish of Rusovce (the Hungarian Oroszvar)

We are familiar with the name Gerulata from Roman historical sources. V. Ondrouch writes that the name Gerulata is found in the Antonine Itinerary and on the Peutinger map of the IVth century A.D. In the Notitia dignitatum occidentis the name of the station is given as Gerolata. The exact location of Gerulata remained for a long time controversial. The Hungarian scholars looked for this station in the region of the then parishes of Rusovce and Jarovce. According to V. Ondrouch even Cunovo parish must be considered.[1] On the Peutinger map Gerulata was marked between Carnuntum and Ad Flexum, which means that it was situated in the territory of the two parishes mentioned.[2] O. Pelikán placed Gerulata without any question in Rusovce. As a result of researches around Bergl, J. Dekan was able to place the Roman Gerulata with certainty in Rusovce.[3] In this study we are concerned neither with the military garrison of Gerulata nor with the civilian settlement in its proximity, but will consider the Roman graves discovered in Rusovce parish.

Archaeological excavations began in Rusovce at the end of the last century. In 1891 the Hungarian scholar A. Sőtér excavated, in the courtyard of house No. 196, a tomb made of bricks decorated with a variety of stamps. By probing in the courtyard he came upon more damaged graves. In the same year he discovered inhumations and a stone tomb[4] in the upper part of the parish. Around the year 1930 a gamekeeper called Főrst allegedly excavated a sacrophagus in the garden of the old school. There are no details of this sarcophagus.[5]

In 1949 archaeologists from the Slovak museum excavated near the local cemetery a child's furnished grave.[6] In 1964 graves were found while building a new school. Later on an excavation was conducted on the site of the school, which continued over several years and which yielded cremations and inhumations (Fig. 2). From 1965 an extensive and systematic research programme was initiated: it was conducted as a joint venture by representatives of the Slovak National Museum and of the Archaeological Institute of the Slovak Academy of Sciences. In 1965-1971 research was concentrated on the re-examination of the structures in the vicinity of Bergl (J. Dekan, A. Piffl) and three Roman burials situated near the school, in the neighbourhood

1

of the cemetery and on the site of JRD (Ľ. Kraskovská, M. Pichlerová).
Within Rusovce parish cremations and inhumations were found in various
places (simple graves, brick and stone tombs and allegedly also a sarcophagus).
The aforesaid cemeteries were used by military garrisons and the civilian
population. The finds in the graves reflected the contemporary culture of the
people and the method of burial testified to the religious beliefs of the population.

The excavations on the site of the new school have now been concluded and
this is why we submit the results of our research to the public as the first
volume of the material from the site of ancient Gerulata.

The finds from the cemetery near the school in Rusovce were recorded
by the members of the Prehistoric Department of the Archaeological Institute,
Slovak National Museum, Bratislava, in the special inventory under the following numbers: 11594-11633, 11861-11886, 12255-12399, 14171-14626.

Finally we would like to thank the administration of the Slovak National
Museum and the administration of the Archaeological Institute for their understanding and for making it possible for us to conduct our research over many
years at Rusovce and for enabling us to publish the results of this research.

We would like to tender our warm thanks to Ms. A. Kováč and Mr. J.
Nettich for their collaboration which made it possible for us to complete this
work. We would like to thank Mr. J. Nettich for drawing up a plan of the
burial ground, Ms. I. Šimekova and Ms. T. Válekova for making photographs
of the finds and Mr. V. Mészároš for drawing the objects.

LOCATION AND HISTORY OF THE SITE

Most of the cemetery was situated on the land of the new nine-year primary school in Rusovce, in the Parish of Bratislava-vidiek (nos. 264-301, Map,fig. 2). The land was slightly elevated and sloped towards the east. The layer of humus was 40-50 cm thick with fine sand underneath. The graves were found between the school-buildings and the gymnasium, in the area of the court-yard behind the gymnasium and on the neighbouring plots of Messrs. J. Hladîk (no. 286), J.R.D. Rusovce (no. 283), Ms. M. Volfova (no. 280) and Ms. M. Klempova (no. 277). However, no graves were found on the neighbouring plots nos. 274 and 271, but on plot no. 271 a damaged object was found. The cemetery occupied a fairly wide strip of ground roughly 30 m long in the east-west direction.

In the Autumn of 1964 while digging the foundations of the gymnasium the workmen came upon inhumations from which they recovered 2 vessels and a bronze brooch. These finds are now in the Slovak National Museum in Bratislava. On the basis of these finds Ms. Pichlerová and J. Nettich, members of the Archaeological Department, re-examined the site and verified the existence of Roman graves. A systematic examination of the burial ground near the school was carried out by the members of the Slovak National Museum in the years of 1965-1969. From the 11-30th October 1965 they excavated the graves nos. 1-5; between May 10th and August 15th, 1966, they found graves nos. 6-10; in 1967 between March 20th and June 1st, and between July 10th and August 12th they excavated graves nos. 11-48; in 1968 they found graves nos. 49-118 between June 3rd and October 15th, finally in 1969 between May 12th and September 19th they examined graves 119-167. Altogether the members of the Slovak National Museum excavated 167 Roman inhumation and cremation graves, and to the east of the burial ground they found a dwelling of Roman date.

ANALYSIS OF THE CREMATION GRAVES

Funeral rites

Cremation graves were ordinary pits without any special embellishment; the exceptions to this were 4 graves covered with Roman bricks. Grave 101 was covered by a brick roof which was originally conical in shape. It was made up of large tegulae (3 are preserved, although there were obviously originally 4). Grave 138 had a flat roof probably made of two tegulae of which only fragments are preserved. Grave 146 was also covered by 2 tegulae, those however were displaced. Grave 69 was covered with 1 tegula. A fragment of brick was found in grave 110, but it is uncertain whether it was used for covering the grave. In grave 107 at a depth of 60 cm there was a gravel base which served as the bottom of the grave. Half of grave 104 was situated on such a gravel base at a depth of 80 cm.

The holes were usually oval or oblong in shape, though some were round in outline. It was not possible to state exactly the outlines and dimensions of the grave pits with 7 of the shallow graves. Before the school was built there were fields and some trees on the site. The layer of humus was comparatively deep (c. 40-50 cm) due to deep ploughing and to tree holes. Some of the cremation graves and finds were in the disturbed level and only by digging deeper was it possible to establish the outline of the grave pit.

Table 1 shows that the cremation graves were typically 30-55 cm deep (this was the case for 59 graves, i.e. almost 80% of the total), the rest of the pits being 60-85 cm deep, except for 3 which were deeper (graves 65, 73 and 94). Grave 73 had the deepest pit, its bottom going down to 110 cm. The objects that were found there (iron plates and remains of locks, nails and fragments of wood), a wooden chest with iron plating show that a scrinium must have been deposited there. The chest contained a glass vessel in perfect condition and a feeding bottle, indicative of a child's grave. There were no traces of bones, only lumps of soil containing ashes. Grave 65 was 105 cm deep; there were 3 vessels of earthenware and one of glass ranged along the wall. There were no fragments of cremated bones here either, only a large piece of charcoal, but judging by the dimensions it could not have been an inhumation. It was presumably a symbolic grave or cenotaph. This assumption is borne out by the fact that the vessels were not in any way affected by fire, not having been on the pyre. The gifts deposited in the grave represent a comparatively unusual collection, not the ordinary offerings: glass, terra sigillata, and a folded beaker.

The average length of the grave-pit was 100-150 cm and the width 90-110 cm. Grave no. 94 was remarkable among the cremation graves in its dimensions; it was 300 cm in length and 180 cm in width. The bottom of the oblong pit was at a depth of 90 cm, and was among the deepest. The walls of the pit were burnt red to a height of 30 cm to such an extent that the contents of the pit had receded from the walls. The burnt soil also extended on the bottom in a 10-40 cm wide strip along the walls. On the bottom and the walls were found traces of wooden piles averaging 15-25 cm in diameter. The bottom was covered mostly by sand except for an area roughly 60 x 60 cm covered in pieces

of carbon and a small group of burnt bones. Fragments of burned objects were
also found, such as a clay lamp, iron and bronze nails, fragments of bronze
plate, and pieces of fused glass. These objects occurred mainly near the walls.

The pit was full of yellow sand in which were found fragments of vessels and
one complete small dish. The centre of the pit was probably cleaned out in-
tentionally as the traces of the pyre were evident only near the walls. Considering this evidence, namely the extraordinarily large dimensions of the pit
and its contents, we assume that it was a place for burning the dead. After
the cremation the remains of the bones together with the residue of the pyre
and fragments of destroyed offerings were placed in the individual graves. It
is noteworthy that the position of grave 94 was near the edge of the cemetery.

There was another pit which had unusual dimensions, being 225 cm long
and 95 cm wide. It probably consisted of two graves but it was not possible
to ascertain their outlines in the disturbed soil and consequently it was marked
as 'grave 123'.

Where cremation graves were concerned we did not notice any regular
rites. The remains of the pyre, cremated bones, pieces of carbon, small
heaps of burnt clay and fragments of objects destroyed in the fire, were
simply tipped into the bottom of the pit. In some of the graves one found only
a small amount of cremated bones and usually only a few damaged gravegoods.
We deduce from this that where cremation was used it was not customary to
bury the entire residue of the funeral pyre, but only a symbolic quantity of
the ashes. It was found that in some cases individual objects were put into the
grave afterwards, as they bore no traces of the effect of fire (e.g. small
glass vessels in graves 72, 73 and 99; a lamp in grave 115; pots in graves
87 and 121). Objects preserved in their entirety were found also in those pits
without any traces of cremated bones, these probably being symbolic graves.
The construction and gravegoods of grave 65 have already been mentioned.
In grave 90 there was a complete small dish of terra sigillata and some potsherds. It was found at a depth of 60 cm so that it is unlikely that it could have
been transferred from another grave by ploughing as it was too deep for that
to happen.

E. Bónis divides cremation graves into urn-graves and pit-graves. In
these instances the dead were cremated at a special place called an ustrinum,
and the remains of the cremated bones were either put into a container or placed
in the grave-pit. A further type were the large cremation graves, busta, where
the dead were cremated directly in the grave-pit. In the 2nd century the custom of burying in urns was in decline. The custom of cremating the dead body
in the grave survived longest in Pannonia.[7] F. Fülep tells us that wooden chests
(scrinia) in which urns and offerings were deposited used to be placed in graves
in the earlier Roman period. The author does not think that the dead were cremated in their graves but in another specially prepared place, the ustrinum. The
hot ashes were poured into a wooden chest, with the offerings on top of the
ashes and then it was placed in the grave-pit.[8] K. Sági, in describing cremation graves in Intercisa, writes that a pyre was erected next to the grave and
the cremated bones, red-hot charcoal and ashes were piled together and
shovelled into the grave-pit. The sides of the pit were therefore burnt to the

height to which the hot remains of the pyre reached. The author considers **busta**, where bodies were cremated in their graves, as a more ancient means of interment.[9] It seems that in Rusovce also hot ashes from the burial place must have been tipped down into the grave as burnt soil was distinctly noticeable at the bottoms of some of the pits. One can assume that, at the Rusovce cemetery, grave 94 was used as the ustrinum. It was not a bustum because the remains of the pyre and the body were not preserved, only a small portion surviving near the walls. The centre of the pit had obviously been cleaned and prepared for the next cremation. One could perhaps call grave 54 a **bustum** as the walls of the pit were fire-reddened and the remains of a cremation lay at the bottom. No urn-graves were found in the cemetery, nor were there any further instances of cremation of the dead in their graves. It would seem probable that wooden chests decorated with iron plating, the remains of which were preserved in graves (nos. 73, 98, 120 and 123), served as **scrinia**. With regard to Rusovce we assume that in two instances the graves were symbolic, namely graves 65 and 90.

In his work on Intercisa, K. Sági lists a cenotaph - a symbolic grave - and at the same time draws our attention to the fact that symbolic interments were not unusual in Roman times.[10]

COINS

Altogether 10 bronze coins were found in the cremation graves in Rusovce; of these 4 were so damaged by fire that it was not possible to identify them precisely: it is only possible to say that they were middle bronzes (graves 69, 87, 97 and 129). The majority of the identifiable coins were of the emperor Hadrian (117-138), namely those in graves 72, 74, 81 and 105. These were all middle bronzes with the reverse type of the figure of a woman, Salus. It is noteworthy that one type of coin in particular was placed in the grave, namely that depicting Salus, good health. This choice probably had something to do with a local custom. The coins of Hadrian were inscribed COS III, this indicating a date of 119 to 138 A.D., a more precise dating of these coins not being possible.

The middle bronze of Faustina from grave 69 was partly damaged by fire and this makes it difficult to determine the exact type. It was probably a coin of Faustina I, wife of Antoninus Pius (A.D. 141). The coin from grave 98 was a middle bronze of Antoninus Pius (138-161) which can be precisely dated to A.D. 148.

GLASS

Glass objects formed an important part of the finds from the cremation graves. Altogether 9 items of glass were found in these graves, representing several types of vessel. Three of these were small zoomorphic vessels in the shape of a bird, which the scholars named tettinae (Säugeflasche). The bottle from grave 73 was made of coarser glass. Two vessels from grave 149 had thin walls, and all were made of green glass (fig. 72, no. 2, 3).

The vessel from grave 73 and the bottle from grave 149 were of similar shape and dimensions (8 cm high), and the second vessel from grave 149 was slightly smaller (c. 6 cm high). The partly fused vessel from grave 68 probably contained either perfume or dye (fig. 72, no. 8). Small bottles with long necks (unguentaria) were used for storing oil; the example from grave 72 was of a flattened globular shape (10 cm high. Fig. 72, no. 1). The long-necked bottle from grave 92 was of conical shape, the rim being broken off so that the original height could not be determined (present height 13.5 cm; fig.72 , no. 4). Judging by its size it could have been part of a set for drinking. A small globular vessel found in grave 105 probably had something to do with toilet articles (height 4.5 cm; fig.72, no. 7). From grave 99 came a square bottle of coarse glass with a short neck and a ribbed handle (height 10.5 cm; fig.72, no.5). The jug from grave 65 was the most beautiful vessel; its round body flowed into the narrow neck and the ribbed handle projected above the rim (height 11 cm; fig. 72 , no. 6). The last two containers were probably used for storing beverages. All the vessels were made either from green or greenish coloured glass. It should be men tioned that with the exception of those from graves 68 and 105 none of the glass vessels had been in the fire: they were placed in the grave-pit afterwards.

Many parallels for the glass vessels have been found in Hungary on military sites and in cremation graves of the Roman period. Small zoomorphic vessels were found in good condition at Brigetio, Intercisa and Aquincum.[11] If we compare the small vessels from Rusovce with the finds from these sites we notice that the vessels from the Rusovce graves were more skilfully executed, especially the one from grave 73. It is possible that all the zoomorphic vessels from Rusovce came from the same glass-works. A. Radnóti writes that the vessels found in the childrens' graves were those used mostly in the 2nd century. L. Barkóczi writes that zoomorphic vessels occurred less frequently in the 2nd century but were also used in the 3rd century.[12]

We find an analogy between the small bottles from the Rusovce cemetery and the glasses from Brigetio dated to the 2nd century. The majority of the glass found in the fort at Brigetio consisted of a variety of little bottles which were of either white, greenish or blueish colour, unguentaria, which were globular or flattened, and those conical in shape. L. Barkóczi described the globular vessels from Brigetio as being for unguents. According to him, flattened round bottles were very wide-spread in the whole of Pannonia (Savaria, Aquincum); bottles with a conical body were found mostly in the region of the Danube, between Carnuntum and Aquincum; small bottles for dyes were used in the south-western part of Pannonia. He states that comparatively few articles of glass were preserved in the graves of the second century due to burial by cremation.[13] At Intercisa various glass bottles were found in cremation graves of the 2nd century. A. Radnóti concludes that the unguentaria were used for perfumes and dyes and that oil was probably stored in the larger bottles with tall necks.[14]

The square bottle with the handle was very similar to the one from Cologne referred to by O. Doppelfeld. It was used for beverages and dated from the 2nd century.[15] The shape of the bottle with the handle and the deep green colour of its glass suggest a western origin; it was probably made in a Rhenish glassworks. Bottles of this type were also found in Pannonia, for example at Brigetio.[16] There is a similarity between the bigger bottle with a tall neck and the articles produced in the Rhineland; we therefore do not exclude the possibility of its having been made there. O. Doppelfeld dates a similar bottle to the 2nd century.[17] The jug with a bulbous body has no exact parallel among the finds from Pannonia. The small vessel with the round body and tall neck is a common type widely used in the 2nd century.[18]

While examining the glass vessels from Intercisa, A. Radnóti sought the origins of the imported glass objects in four different areas: in Egypt, Asia Minor, Syria and the Rhineland. The author assumes that the perfume and oil bottles originated in the East, mostly Syria, and found their way to Pannonia through trading. We assume that the glass was usually transported by water.[19] L. Barkóczi stated that the small vessels from Brigetio dated from the 2nd century. He writes that, besides the imports from Italy, glass articles were also imported from the west, and that articles from eastern workshops were found among them. He presumes that there were glass-works in Pannonia as early as the 2nd century. Although we do not recognise the articles of local manufacture and cannot identify them, we must recognise their existence. He considers the small simple bottles of inferior material and of imperfect workmanship to have been made locally. He indicates that the workshops could have been in Aquincum, a view based on the glass finds.[20] As we can see, the Hungarian scholars did not succeed in solving the question of the origins of the individual types of vessel in spite of the great numbers of glass objects that were discovered. The small number of glass vessels from Rusovce did not help in resolving this question.

LAMPS

Small earthenware oil-lamps were frequently found in the Rusovce graves. Thirty lamps and 6 lamp-fragments, 36 pieces altogether, were preserved in the cemetery. The entire lamps were from 2 to 3.5 cm high, their average height being 2.5-2.8 cm. The length of the lamps varied between 6.5 and 10.5 cm, half of them being 8.5-9 cm long. The average diameter of the upper surface of the lamps was 4.4 to 7.2 cm, the majority averaging 5-6 cm. The colour was not uniform; most were grey (16 lamps) with some yellow ones and some red or brown. On some of the lamps there were traces of a slip, mostly in red (graves 60, 87, 96 and 125), and in some cases traces of a yellow and brown slip (graves 66, 72, 74, 75 and 164). Excavators have often studied the clay lamps frequently found on Roman sites. The basic classification of lamps according to types was made by S. Loeschcke in his work on lamps from the Roman fort at Vindonissa.[21] D. Iványi has written a work on lamps from Pannonia, and she has extended the classification made by S. Loeschke.[22] A considerable number of lamps were found on the immense Roman site at Intercisa; a work on these was written by K. Póczy in which she used the typology of D. Iványi.[23] More recently T. Szentléleky has published a work on Roman lamps, working out his own typology but referring to the types of S. Loeschcke and D. Iványi .[24] A. Neumann discussed the lamps in the Roman camp of Vindobona and used D. Iványi's classification. He considered most of the factory-made lamps that were found there to be typical provincial products of local workshops; he included among these lamps with a glossy slip, colour-coated and ones with a rough surface.[25]

When analysing the clay lamps from the Rusovce cemetery we have used S. Loeschcke's classification but we refer at the same time to the relevant type according to the system of D. Iványi. Both scholars defined two basic groups: lamps with relief decoration and "mass-produced" lamps (Bildlampen, Firmalampen). The first group can be more precisely characterised as lamps with volutes and those with a relief.

Only one lamp representative of the first group was found in Rusovce, namely in grave 104. It is decorated with volutes around the opening for the wick and with a relief of a fish on the disc; and the opening for oil is asymmetrically placed. This lamp belongs to Loeschcke's type I.[26] T. Szentléleky informs us that the commonest type was a variant of type IC. He lists as type IC a similar lamp with a fish relief. According to T. Szentléleky's description, the lamp from Rusovce grave 104 also belonged to type IC. The author writes that this type of lamp with the fish relief belongs approximately to the 1st century; it was produced in the reign of the emperor Tiberius (after A.D. 37). Lamps of this type were used in Pannonia until the middle of the 2nd century.[27] D. Iványi depicts similar lamps with volutes and a fish relief that were found on Roman sites in Hungary (Szombathely, Györ, Sopron) and this type dates in Pannonia to the 1st and 2nd centuries. A lamp with this type of decoration was found at Carnuntum.[28] Lamps decorated in relief only rarely had a stamp at the bottom.[29] The lamp from Rusovce grave 104 represents an older type of lamp with volutes and relief decoration and can be dated to the transition from the 1st to the 2nd centuries.

All the other lamps that were found near the school belonged to the "mass-produced" type. Compared with the lamps with relief decoration, these lamps were simpler and from the practical point of view more functional as sources of light. According to T. Szentléleky they came into use after A.D. 70, at the beginning of the Flavian period. For two centuries they were the predominant type in Italy and in the Danube provinces.[30] Most of them had a stamp with a Latin inscription on the base; such stamps were used from the end of the 1st century. D. Iványi thinks that initially the stamps bore the name of the individual potter, and later that of the factory.

Among such lamps from the graves at Rusovce we can distinguish, following the classification of S. Loeschcke, types IX and X, which are different in their arrangement of the channel for the oil.[32] The upper surface of lamp type IX has two variants. In the first there was a narrow moulded border around the disc, and on the neck between the disc and the opening for the wick there was a narrow groove; in the second, the strip on the neck was interrupted and formed a narrow projection which did not quite reach the opening for the wick. On lamps of type X the moulded strip forming a rim around the disc continued further onto the neck and formed a rim around the opening for the wick. One or two small openings were sometimes placed between the strip which formed a rim round the neck.

An older type of the "mass-produced" lamps of type IX (Iványi's type XV) was represented by 3 specimens from Rusovce (graves 66, 72 and 80); one of them had no marks, but the other two bore the stamp FORTIS.[33] According to S. Loeschcke lamps of type IX were produced from A.D. 75 to 100. D. Iványi modified this dating for Pannonia, where lamps of type IX were used until the end of the 2nd century. A. Neumann dated some of these types from Vindobona to the end of the 1st century.[34] The lamps of type IX which were found in Rusovce can be dated to the first half of the second century. The dating is supported by the finding in grave 72 of a coin of Hadrian (117-138) together with a lamp of this type.

The most widely used trade-mark was the stamp FORTIS, which is also reported by S. Loeschcke, D. Iványi, T. Szentléleky and K. Póczy.[35] T. Szentleleky writes that Fortis worked in Northern Italy, in the neighbourhood of Modena.[36] Around 70 (or, according to S. Loeschcke, around 100) Fortis perfected the "mass-produced" type of lamp, Loeschcke's type X or Iványi's type XVII.[37] This type of lamp was not changed further and continued to be produced in the 2nd and 3rd centuries. D. Iványi considers that this type of lamp was used in Pannonia from the last decade of the 1st century to the middle of the 4th century. She also says that in the beginning the Pannonian copies of the Italian originals were meticulously made of good material and the letters on the stamps were carefully moulded and prominent. The stamps on the early lamps were also larger. With the later stamps the fabric and workmanship deteriorated and the letters became coarse and ill-defined.[38]

Most of the lamps (27) found at Rusovce belonged to Loeschcke's type X. One, from grave 108, was a variant of type X with a short neck, classified by D. Iványi as her type XVII. The lamp from grave 108 differed from the other examples not only in its shape but also by the marking: on the base were printed the letters RN in retrograde. We do not find this type of stamp on the lamps in Hungary according to D. Iványi or K. Póczy.

The mass-produced lamps were usually undecorated. However, one group of lamps of Type X was decorated on the disc with a moulded head. A lamp of this type was found in grave 115 at Rusovce (Pl. V, no. 15). The disc was decorated with a moulded mask and at the sides were two small openings for oil. The mask is worked in fine detail and in high relief. It should be noted that this lamp bearing a stamp of FORTIS in high relief was distinguished from the others by its excellent workmanship. The lamp from grave 125 was probably similar. Traces of a moulded decoration, possibly of a head, can be seen on the lamp from grave 60. Both these lamps were stamped FORTIS and had traces on their sides of a red shiny slip.

Lamps decorated with a moulded head are illustrated by D. Iványi. We do not find here an exact parallel with the lamp from grave 115, but one of the lamps from Szombathely belongs to this type and the one from Eisenstadt has a similar mask.[39] The lamp with a mask from grave 115 and two others with a relief of a head found at Rusovce belonged to a type of decorated lamp well known in Pannonia.

Mass-produced lamps of Type X had a variety of stamps. In Rusovce the most widely used stamp was the one of the FORTIS factory, which was found on eleven lamps (graves 60, 74, 103, 110, 115, 125, 129, 146, 149 and 156). Smaller numbers of the following stamps was found: AGILIS F (grave 87) CPSF (grave 129), FESTI (graves 81 and 117), LNARI (grave 94), PULLI (grave 163), SCA (grave 97), VIBIUS (graves 99 and 121) and traces of a stamp IER (grave 132; fig. 75 nos. 1-23). This was probably the stamp NERI which was found on a lamp from Vindobona.[40] On the base of one of the lamps there was an engraved inscription (grave 129). Only 5 lamps of Type X were unstamped (graves 54, 68, 98, 105 and 164).

All these stamps are mentioned in articles on stamps from Pannonia. D. Iványi mentions the stamps AGILIS F and CPSF five times, FESTI fifteen times, LNARI 22 times, PULLI 7 times, VIBIUS twice, and SCA three times.[41]

The lamps of Type X from Rusovce cemetery can be dated to the 2nd century. This dating is based on the associated finds. The lamps of this type were found in graves 74, 81 and 105 with coins of Hadrian (A.D. 117-138) and in grave 98 with a coin of Antoninus Pius (138-161). If we accept the assertion of D. Iványi that the earlier lamps had a large stamp in high relief, then the lamps from graves 75, 97, 99, 110, 115, 121 and 156 were of the early type.[42] According to this, the rest of the lamps with the small stamps in lower relief were of the second half of the 2nd century.

One item is prominent among the lamps from the Rusovce cemetery, namely a fragment of a lamp with a figure of a horse. The bowl for the oil is missing and only part of the figure remains, which served as a handle (Pl. VI, no. 8). There is a close parallel in a complete lamp found in

of the potter was correctly read. The letter H is quite clear so that it could not have been the stamp STABILIS which W. Ludowici mentions from Rheinzabern. It was probably a different stamp from Rheinzabern which Ludowici quotes as MABILISF.[53]

One sherd was decorated by part of a human figure with a garland and the fore-part of a horse (fig. 76, no. 3). It is probably a sea-horse (hippocampus). We find analogous figures on vessels found at Lezoux. G. Juhasz illustrates among the finds from Brigetio sherds with a garland and a figure of a sea-horse similar to those from Lezoux. There was another design on the Lezoux sherds from Brigetio, a human form and a hand.[54] From the quoted examples we identify the patterned terra sigillata sherd as coming from Lezoux. K. Póczy mentions that in Aquincum there was a branch of the Lezoux workshop which was burnt down between the years 120-130.[55] We do not know whether the sherd came from a locally-made or imported vessel.

The rest of the fragments probably belonged to one vessel. A Dragendorff form 37 dish was reconstructed from them, the sides of which were divided into panels some of which contained medallions probably 2 in number (fig. 76 no. 5). In one of the medallions there is the head of a horse. Another probably came from a vessel with ovolos and panels below, but it was not possible to reconstruct the decoration in detail from the few surviving fragments (fig. 76, no. 1). Another small fragment was decorated with ovolos (fig. 76 no. 6). The fragments were insufficient for a reconstruction, and did not enable us to say where the vessel had been made. The only indication of its origin was from the general design and the fabric: it was most probably made at Rheinzabern.

The last fragment of terra sigillata, from burial 7, was decorated with ovolos and the head of a feline (fig. 76, no. 2). We find this type of decoration on dishes from Rheinzabern and Westerndorf. A similar head was found on a fragment from Brigetio with the stamp of potter ATTONI from Rheinzabern.[56] One cannot exclude the possibility that fragment from burial 7 came from this workshop.

It is evident from the analysis of the fragments of terra sigillata from the Rusovce cemetery that the majority of the vessels were produced at Rheinzabern (graves 65, 87 and some other fragments). The fragment with the figure-design probably came from Lezoux.

POTTERY

The pottery found with the burials shows on the whole a uniform character. It is obvious that only certain types of vessel were used for ritual purposes and we cannot therefore tell from the finds in the cemetery what types were actually in daily use. All the vessels were made on a fast rotating potter's wheel and fired in special kilns. We can divide the vessels found in the burials into groups according to fabric, form and decoration.

The vessels of grey fabric with a rough surface formed a separate group and these can be sub-divided into several types. The commonest type in the burials was a small wide-mouthed jar, the neck decorated with grooves widening out into a horizontal rim. The height of these pots was 6.5-9.4 cm, the maximum diameter was 9-12.5 cm and the diameter of the base 3-5 cm.

Four complete pots of this type were found (burials 54, 59, 99 and 159) and 7 fragments, 11 pieces in all (fig. 77, no. 5, 6, 7). Besides the small pots which could be used for drinking, a large undecorated pot was found in burial 151 (height 16.5 cm) and in grave 72 a rim fragment of a still larger pot was found (fig. 77, no. 11).

A common form was the folded beaker. Two such vessels in grey fabric were found in the burials in Rusovce and it was established that there are 2 types. The beaker from burial 65 had a tall narrow body with 6 indentations (height 26.5 cm); that from burial 121 was wider, of spherical shape (height 13 cm) (fig. 77, nos. 8, 9). Their straight rims were decorated with lines. Two fragments of similar beakers were found (burials 111 and 161). There was also a second type of folded beaker at Rusovce and we will describe this in detail in connection with the fine pottery.

A large vessel from burial 99 of grey fabric represented another type of vessel. It differed considerably from the jugs in its wide neck and its spout, and by its rounded handle (height 21 cm) (fig. 77, no. 10).

Another group consisted of vessels of a yellow fabric with a smooth surface made of fine alluvial clay. The jugs were tall with egg-shaped bodies and a narrow neck finished off with a funnel-like rim; the strip-like handle was often decorated with grooves. Certain variations in form and size were noticeable with these jugs, but they formed a single type. For the complete examples the height of the jugs varied from 22 cm to 33 cm, the diameter of the rim from 5 to 7 cm (though some larger jugs were found with a diameter of 10 cm), the maximum diameter from 12 cm to 19 cm and the base diameter 5-7.6 cm. Five of these yellow jugs were preserved (burials 27, 59, 74, 81 and 110) and 40 fragments (fig. 78, nos. 1, 2). To these we should add 4 similar jugs in red fabric, making a total of 49. Since 83 graves were excavated in the cemetery, in which there were 49 jugs, this type of vessel was present in 60% of the burials: tall yellow jugs were the commonest type of vessel in the cemetery.

A small jug from burial 109 was unusual. It also had an egg-shaped body
with a narrow neck which continued into a funnel-like spout (height 10.4 cm)
(fig. 78, no. 4). The jug from burial 160 differed from the tall jugs in its
wider conical neck which was continuous with the egg-shaped body on a short
stem (height 19 cm).

From the yellow alluvial clay small dishes were also made. They were
either conical or hemispherical in shape, and their rims were reinforced.
The fragments indicated that they were 3-5 cm in height and 8 cm in diameter.
Five fragments of the yellow clay fabric were found, and one fragment of red
colour (burials 78, 92, 112, 113, 115 and 117. Of a similar red colour were
two cylindrical stems belonging to small pots, the shape of which could not be
determined (burial 100). Among the yellow sherds was one type which was not
present in the burials but unstratified fragments of which were found. It was
a so-called censer (Rauchgefäss): a wide dish with sloping sides on a tall stem
with richly moulded decoration on the sides of the dish. The rims of the dishes
were slashed and below, on the sides, were attached similarly slashed cordons
(table VI, no. 9). Yellow or grey-yellow fragments of six dishes made of this
clay were found. It was not possible to reconstruct the dishes from the fragments, but the type is known to us from other sites.

From burials 78 and 107 came perforated sherds from some kind of sieve
made of yellow clay (Pl. VI, no. 6). It was not possible to establish the form
of the vessel more closely and E. Bónis[57] does not quote any analogies.

A group of vessels made of yellow clay with a red colour coat is connected
with the yellow fabric types described above. The folded beaker in yellow fabric
colour-coated red all over (fig. 77, no. 12) was related to the beakers discussed above. From burial 92 there came an egg-shaped pot with a horizontal
rim, which bore traces of red colour-coating on a vermilion clay (fig. 78,
no. 3). There were traces of some red colour-coating on a fragment of a
globular vessel on a stem from burial 129. A fragment of a vessel on a
narrow foot-ring from burial 114 differed from the other colour-coated vessels
in that the body was decorated with a wavy red line.

The red colour-coated vessels were imitations of the costly terra sigillata.
The shape of the dish in grave 78 was hemispherical with a small foot-ring.
On the inside of the base was a stamp without an inscription in planta pedis.
It was the largest well-preserved dish in the cemetery (diameter 27 cm).
Only fragments survived of other examples, which suggested that the dishes
had either sloping or vertical sides (burials 75, 94, 96, 101, 116 and 153).

In addition there were a few individual vessels of various types which
formed part of the inventory of the burials. The vessel from grave 90 had
an unusual ornamentation. There was a brown colour-coating over the
yellow clay which bore traces of Garbotine applique. The fragment of a folded
beaker from grave 78 made of red clay with a silvery coating was decorated en
barbotine. In this grave there was found a fragment of a red globular cup with
a handle which was much finer than the other vessels. Grave 65 yielded a
unique find: a globular beaker with a conical neck; on the convex part it was

17

decorated by fine incisions. It was very thin, very well fired, and covered with a black shiny coating (fig. 78, no. 6). The shallow dish from grave 94 was 17 cm in diameter (fig. 78, no. 5). E. Bónis has discussed the type in Pannonia in the earlier Roman times and made an analysis of the various types of vessel.[58] She took as her starting point the pottery of the 1st century but found that these forms also continued into the 2nd century. She divided the vessels according to their forms, not according to their fabrics. Various types of vessel from the Rusovce burials bear many similarities to the vessels found in the rest of Pannonia. We will follow the order in which we dealt with the vessels from Rusovce.

E. Bónis called a small grey cup a "beaker" and gave this name to all the vessels up to 15 cm in height. This form was fairly widespread on other localities and she mentions pots of similar form and dimensions from the sites in Sopron, Keszthelyi and Petronella.[59] The folded beakers illustrated by her were characterized by smaller dimensions; they were usually up to 12 cm in height and only a few were higher. We find among these both shapes found in Rusovce, namely the tall and the globular beaker.[60] Bonis looks for the origins of the folded beakers among the glass vessels. In the earlier Roman times the beakers were smaller, and later on larger ones with coarse grey surfaces became popular. The grey jugs with spouts found at Rusovce bear a close resemblance to the vessels found at Carnuntum, Eisenstadt, Szombathelyi and Keszthelyi.[61]

We mentioned that the most widely distributed type found in the Rusovce burials was the tall, narrow-necked jug made of yellow clay. E. Bónis illustrates several types of these jugs of which she lists about 50 similar vessels, thus confirming the popularity of this type in the whole of Pannonia.[62] Similar jugs were found even in Noricum, where they were used in the 2nd and 3rd centuries, as is demonstrated by examples quoted by E. Schörgendorfer.[63]

Bonis quotes many examples of censers decorated in different ways found in burials in Pannonia. She concludes that it is impossible to date this vessel as it was used in different modifications until the end of the Roman era. They were made in considerable quantities in Pannonia in the 2nd century. According to A. Schörgendorfer the censers were in circulation in Austria in the frontier areas up to Carnuntum, and are found on sites occupied by the Roman garrisons.[64] He assumes that their function was probably connected with some ritual. They are found in Austria from the middle of the 2nd century up to the 4th century. In Rusovce fragments of these censers were found in an actual grave. We assume that this type of vessel was most certainly used for ritual purposes, like the lamps, or perhaps for burning of aromatic substances. The censers were probably placed over the grave after the funeral or at some sort of requiem celebrations.

We described the small dishes from graves 78 and 90 as imitations of terra sigillata. A.Schörgendorfer describes imitations of terra sigillata as vessels, usually small dishes, coloured red on their surface and lightly fired. The clay of these vessels quickly became soft in the earth and they began to fall apart.[65] These characteristics also apply to the small dishes from Rusovce. Bónis writes that the stamp in planta pedis was used in Pannonia for a longer time on the imitations of terra sigillata than on the original types of these vessels. This type of stamp was used by potters of the 2nd century, but usually without the name of the maker.[66]

The decoration on the sherd from burial 90 can be described as en barbotine. Schörgendorfer dates a vessel with barbotine ornament and a yellow-brown colour-coat to the 1st to 2nd century.[67] Bónis describes small folded beakers with a red colour-coat and decorated en barbotine; however, she does not date them as this type was used until the end of the Roman period. According to Schörgendorfer the barbotine decoration on drinking vessels was especially common in the 1st and 2nd centuries, and began to decline at the end of the 2nd century.[68] The small vessel with the black coating from burial 65 is very similar to one found in Austria dated to the middle of the 2nd century. A. Mócsy considers a similar small black vessel from a burial at Szombathelyi to be a western importation (the cemetery was dated to the first half of the 2nd century).[69] This fine pot, represented by a few vessels, was probably not manufactured in Pannonia but was imported from the west.

An analysis of the pottery found in the cemetery at Rusovce shows that the greater part was manufactured in the local workshops in Pannonia (the grey and yellow fabrics and the red colour-coated vessel). In addition to these, there were vessels which were different in form and fabric and which can be considered as imports (e.g. the small vase from burial 65, and the vessel from burial 90). The dating of these vessels is based on their parallels from Pannonia. The forms in grey fabric (the cup, the folded beaker, and the jug) referred to by Bónis correspond to similar vessels from an earlier Roman era; this means that they belonged to the 2nd century. This forms the basis for dating the pot from the Rusovce burials to the 2nd century.

K. Póczy has written on the history and the products of the pottery workshops of Aquincum. So far six centres of pottery manufacture have been discovered in various places. The workshops in Aquincum produced pottery from the beginning of the 2nd century to the middle of the 3rd century. Besides other types they made small dishes in imitation of terra sigillata, censers, and tall jugs of yellow clay. Póczy also mentions the pottery factories at Brigetio which were operating in the first half of the 2nd century.[70] So far we have not been able to attribute the vessels found in the burials at Rusovce to individual workshops, as this entails studies of material abroad. It is quite possible, however, that some vessels were imported from the workshops referred to.

ORNAMENTS

Most of the ornaments were destroyed during cremation, and only remnants were preserved in the burials. In burials 92, 94 and 129 pieces of fused glass were found. A fragment of a bronze brooch was found in burial 69; judging by the fragment, which was part of the spring and bow, it was a brooch with a high fastening (fig.85 , no. 18). The high fastening was common to brooches of several types. It is impossible to date the brooch precisely: M. Lamiová says that it is very difficult to date them closely as they were in use from the end of the 1st to the end of the 3rd centuries . She dated the finds from Slovakia to the 2nd and 3rd centuries. The fragments of the brooch from the cremation can therefore be dated to the 2nd century.

In burial 92 fragments were found of an ornament made of bronze plates; all the fragments seem to come from one object. There were two end-pieces of the ornament in the shape of a narrow tube and a fragment of tube widened in the middle (Plate IV, no. 7). We can assume from the fragments that it was an ornamental necklet, widened in the middle and tapering to smooth ends. No parallels are known from Pannonia.

In graves 68 and 94 there were small fragments of bronze plates. In grave 96 there was a curved bronze plate, probably from a sheath (Plate IV, no. 8). In grave 69 there was an ornamental bronze plate in the shape of a rectangle with volutes at either end (fig. 85, no. 19). Judging from the shape, it was probably the plate for a key-hole belonging to a chest which had been burned. It had been scorched but had not melted. The open work iron plate from grave 121 was a unique find; its centre was filled by a star-shaped design made of bronze wire (fig. 85, no. 20), but there were no holes for any threads nor were there eyelets for a fastening, so its shape or function remains uncertain. The technique of its manufacture suggests that it could have carried an enamel decoration.

PLATED BOXES

In some of the burials fragments of iron plating were found, parts of locks and nails which were remnants of burned boxes called <u>scrinia</u>. The most complete remains of a box were those preserved in grave 73; tin plating for a key-hole, the inside of a lock, hinges for the lid and various pieces of narrow iron bands which were probably from the outside of the box. It was not possible to reconstruct the box from the surviving fragments, but it was obvious from the size of the bands and the key-hole plate (11 x 10 cm) and the length of hinges (10 cm) that the box was comparatively large. It was locked by means of a fairly complicated lock. The key was not found but judging by the construction of the lock it had a serrated tongue. It was not possible to ascertain whether the narrow iron bands served to strengthen the chest or whether they were purely ornamental.

In burial 120 there were also found iron plates from a wooden box, namely a tinned plate, probably for a key-hole, an oblong-shaped tinned piece, probably the spring from a lock, and hinges from the lid. Even in this case it was impossible to determine the size of the box. Iron fragments which were preserved in burials 73 and 120 were undoubtedly the remains of wooden boxes. The plates from other burials did not have such typical features (part of a lock, plating for a key-hole), but it is quite probable that they came from <u>scrinia</u>.

From burial 95 came fragments of iron bindings with rivets in the corners: there was one larger piece which must have originally been 11 cm long and a smaller fragment of another strip. In cremation 123 there was a larger oblong plate (14 cm long) which did not have rivet holes. It was not possible to ascertain the use of a massive iron ring with 2 rivets (diam. <u>c</u>. 10 cm), found in a cremation grave. Similar iron plates were found in burials 105 and 76, onto which were fastened narrow strips by means of eyelets. These plates had neither rivet holes nor eyelets for fastenings. It was probably part of an iron lock.

A considerable number of wooden boxes with metal plates were found in Intercisa, but in contrast to those from Rusovce the plates were for the most part made of bronze and not iron. A. Radnóti analysed the bronze plates and divided them into several groups. In some of the burials the wood was also preserved, which made it possible to assess the sizes of the boxes. From the wood remains and plates it was possible to reconstruct the heights and lengths of the boxes but not the widths. On the basis of these measurements Radnóti gives the height of the wooden boxes as 22-32 cm, and their length as 24-40 cm.[72] One can regard them as small portable chests with an average height of 25 cm and an average length of 30 cm. Wooden boxes were usually found in women's burials and judging by the finds they usually contained toilet implements and ornaments. Radnóti did not examine in detail the iron locks; he mentions, however, that the locks had an internal sliding part. The serrated keys belonged to this type of lock.[73]

A. Salamon examined the iron plates from wooden chests from Intercisa. She illustrated fragments of these plates and parts of the locks in her article.[74] The lock found at Rusovce in burial 73 was most likely constructed in the same way as the lock found in Intercisa.

Fragments of iron plates from cremation burials 73 and 120 proved that wooden boxes (scrinia) with iron locks and plates were used in Rusovce cemetery.

IRON OBJECTS

Iron nails of varying sizes, usually with a flat head, were present in many cremation burials. They occurred in comparatively small numbers, 1 to 5 per grave. Among these there were nails 9-13 cm long which were probably used for fastening the pile of wood at the actual cremation, and nails 4-7.5 cm long some of which were used for the building of the pile of wood and some of which came from plain wooden chests in which the ashes from the cremation were placed. The smaller nails (2-3.5 cm long) were, no doubt, used for the same purpose. Iron nails were found in one third of the burials.

Iron rivets with an average length of 1.5 cm, and with hemispherical heads, were also present in these cremation burials. There were usually 3 to 6 of them in a grave, depending on what was left over from the cremation and tipped into the pit. In only two burials was there a larger quantity of rivets, namely in burial 68 where there were 15, and in burial 95 where there were 36. Iron rivets were found in 15 cremation graves (68, 69, 74, 94, 95, 96, 107, 112, 125, 126, 131, 132, 141, 146 and 162). In burial 94 there was also found a small bronze rivet. We will describe the use of iron rivets in more detail when analysing the inhumations, in which rivets were found in considerable quantities.

Only one complete iron knife was found (in cremation burial 108) which had a pointed blade and an incomplete iron handle (length 15.5 cm). In burial 112 there was a fragment of a small, straight knife - blade 9 cm long.

THE DATING OF THE CREMATION BURIALS

The cremation burials in Rusovce cemetery formed roughly half of the excavated graves. Examination of the cremations shows that there was a uniform method of burial. The remains of the cremation were tipped into a fairly large grave-pit, and some of the grave-goods were put into the burial afterwards. A few graves were exceptions to this rule, for example, burials 65 and 90 which were probably cenotaphs, and burial 94 which obviously served as a place for cremation.

The dating of the cremation graves is based on the finds of the coins and some types of grave-goods which are easily dated, such as lamps, terra sigillata and perhaps small glass vessels. The coins found in the burials dated from A.D. 117-148, indicating that these burials mostly dated from the second quarter of the 2nd century. The clay lamps were represented by a few types which belonged to the first and second half of the 2nd century. The terra sigillata was dated by the stamps to the 2nd century. One can be dated more precisely to the middle of the 2nd century. On the strength of analogous finds from Pannonia, the small glass vessels also dated from the 2nd century. We may conclude that all the datable finds were of the 2nd century; consequently the Rusovce cemetery can be dated to the 2nd century A.D. The fashion of cremation carried on in other cemeteries in Pannonia until the middle of the 3rd century, and it is quite possible that individual cremations at Rusovce could be from the 3rd century although they did not contain any grave-goods which would have enabled us to determine their date more precisely.

ANALYSIS OF THE INHUMATIONS

THE FUNERAL RITES

Inhumations in the Rusovce cemetery were carried out in two ways; either in constructed tombs or in simple graves . Eight tombs of brick or stone were found, which can be divided into several types. First they may be divided into the ones made of brick and the ones built of stone; they also differed from one another by the shape of the roof which was either conical or flat.

Grave 2 was the most complicated and carefully constructed of all. The long side walls were formed by mortared tegulae, and the end walls were built of mortared stone and raised above the level of the ground. A conical roof rested on them, built of tegulae and imbrices. The base of the tomb was made up of large square bricks. The other brick tomb, no. 43, had the side walls made of bricks and fragments of tegulae bonded with clay and not with mortar; the ends were formed by single tegulae and the bottom was covered with bricks of various widths (28-58 cm). In contrast to this grave, number 43 had a flat roof made of 3 square bricks and their fragments. The child's tomb, no. 11, was also built in this way but only tegulae were used here. There were 6 bricks on the sides, three on the bottom and three more formed the flat roof.

Other grave chambers were built from stone bonded with mortar or clay. Grave 39 had walls 20 cm thick, and the floor was made of 4 large bricks. The conical roof was made of tegulae and imbrices. The construction of the roof was the same as that of grave 2, but the side walls were not raised; the gaps above them were covered by tegulae which in turn held the imbrices. Two other graves had the same construction with a flat roof. The walls of grave 13 were made of stone bonded with clay and not mortar; on their edges rested a frame made of fragments of bricks. The floor was covered by a large stone and 2 tegulae. The flat roof was formed by tegulae. The sides of tomb 36 were built from stone and fragments of brick bonded with mortar. Around the edge there was a frame of stones and fragments of bricks and on this rested the roof. The floor was covered by 3 oblong bricks. The flat roof was made of 3 bricks and some large stones.

Graves 5 and 20 were of a simpler type. The walls of grave 5, just like grave 36, were constructed of stone bonded with mortar, and on the top edge there rested a frame made of fragments of bricks. However, there were no bricks on the floor, and the body lay directly on the sand. The flat roof was made of three bricks and a large stone. For the construction of tomb 20, 4 square bricks were used; of these three were standing at the head and the fourth by the feet; what remained of the side walls was constructed of stone and clay. The floor was formed by the natural subsoil. Nothing remained of the roof. There were some indications of a brick tomb in grave 21: there was one brick on either of the cross-walls by the head and feet. We assume a similar arrangement in tomb 6 which was damaged.

It is evident from this description that three types of brick were used for the construction of the tombs: large square bricks (60 x 60 cm), tegulae (50 x 40 cm), and imbrices 40 cm long. The bricks used for military constructions were marked by stamps of the appropriate legion. These stamped bricks were a help in dating. The greater part of bricks used for the construction of tombs in Rusovce were unstamped. Stamped bricks were preserved in only 3 tombs: in tomb 6 there was a tegula bearing a stamp of Legio XIV. The greatest number of stamped bricks was preserved in tomb 36: one tegula with a damaged stamp (probably Legio XIV), and 2 square bricks marked with the stamp of Legio XIV Gemina. A square brick with the same stamp was used in tomb 43. We note that all the marked bricks bore the stamp of Legio XIV Gemina; such bricks were found in considerable numbers on the site of a Roman building at Bergl, and Legio XIV Gemina was stationed in Gerulata up to the 2nd century.[75] Material from older buildings was probably used for the construction of 4th century graves, which would explain the occurrence of stamped bricks in this later context.

Originally the graves were sunk in the earth so that only the roofs were visible on the surface. It is evident from the description above that there was some variation in their construction. We also notice a certain variation in the dimensions of these tombs, in the dimension of the tomb proper and in the roof. The length of the grave chamber was from 155 cm to 195 cm, the width 35-55 cm and the depth 30-50 cm. The lengths of the flat roofs were commensurate with the dimensions of the tomb (170-205 cm), but the conical roofs overlapped the tombs proper on all sides (length 200-235 cm, width 90-95 cm).

Burial in constructed tombs was certainly more expensive than in ordinary grave-pits and it is only logical to expect to find in them the richest finds, but the Rusovce graves offered quite a different picture. Grave 2 contained a great variety of grave-goods; the occupant, a woman, was buried with ornaments, 6 coins, glass vessels for toilet purposes and pots. It was obviously the undisturbed original inhumation. Nor was the child's tomb (no. 11), in which were found a coin and two vessels, disturbed. Tomb 20 had no roof, but the skeleton was completely preserved and a bronze brooch was in situ; consequently we also consider this inhumation to have been undisturbed. Part of grave 13 had been damaged by a tree hole which had destroyed the lower limbs; there were no finds in the preserved part of the inhumation. Part of tomb 39 was also damaged at the lower end; there remained only fragments of the skull and bones and insignificant fragments of grave-goods. Here it is difficult to decide whether the tomb was damaged and robbed in Roman times or destroyed at a later period.

In the graves mentioned so far there was always only one person buried. In tomb 36 there was an undamaged skeleton without grave-goods, and in the corner of the grave by its feet were piled together the grave-goods (bracelets, a glass vase and 2 small pots).[76]

An even more complicated situation was found in grave 5. There was a complete skeleton, and near its skull there was placed another skull and the bones of a second skeleton, and by the feet were found the skull and bones of a third skeleton: besides the buried person the remains of two inhumations were placed in the tomb. Only a bone comb was found near the first skeleton, in addition to a metal plate belonging probably to an earlier burial. It can be assumed in these cases (graves 5 and 36) that they were family tombs. In both these tombs there were no grave-goods with the most recently buried skeleton; we assume this to be the influence of Christianity on the burial rites of the population. According to A. Radnóti a lot of Christians were buried in the cemtery at Intercisa in the 4th century. [77] In the last tomb (no. 43) the bones were piled up in one part of the grave, but the skull and gifts were absent. One can assume that the tomb prepared for a further burial, though it is surprising that the skull and grave-goods were removed. The possibility remains that the grave might have been robbed.

The orientations of the skeletons in the constructed tombs and their positions did not differ from those of the skeletons in the simple grave pits. In tombs 2, 5, 13, 20 and 39 the skeleton lay with the head turned towards the north-west; in tomb 11 the head was turned west; in tomb 36 the body and head were directed towards the north-east. The surviving skeletons lay in an extended position, and their hands were either alongside the body or on the lap; only in tomb 20 did the hands of the skeleton lie on the waist.

The bones from the burials were not examined anatomically, and so the sex of the persons buried in the graves was determined by the grave-goods. A woman was, no doubt, buried in grave 2. Judging by the measurements, grave 11 was that of a child. The brooch found in grave 20 indicated that the skeleton was that of a man. The skeletons in graves 39 and 43 were destroyed, and there were no finds in grave 13 where the skeleton was partly destroyed. There were no characteristic finds with the well-preserved skeletons in the family graves 5 and 36, but judging by the bones they were women's skeletons.

Similar tombs made of brick or of stone with roofs of various types of construction were excavated at several Roman sites in Pannonia. To quote some examples: in the cemetery at Budapest (Becsi utca) there were tombs made of bricks, of stone slabs or of stone with flat or conical roofs made of brick. G. Parragi puts the date of the cemetery from the middle to the end of the 4th century. [78] Also in the other cemetery at Budapest, in Aquincum, there were tombs made of bricks or of stone slabs. [79] In the brick-built tomb in Budapest (Bogdáni utca) together with an onion-shaped brooch there was a coin of Constantius II. [80] In Szekszárde a brick tomb with a conical roof contained similar objects. [81] In Tác (Roman Gorsium), in the cemetery at Margittelepi there were found tombs of types which were known at Rusovce: tombs made of bricks, those built of stones and fragments of bricks, covered by conical or flat roofs. V. Lányi dates this cemetery to the middle of the 4th century. [82] J. Fitz dated the Roman cemetery at Csakvár (Floriana) to the second half of the 4th century; there was a tomb there made of bricks with a flat roof. [83]

To sum up, we can see that the Hungarian scholars dated the tombs built in brick to the 4th century, and mostly to its second half. In the sites referred to, adjacent tombs were built from brick or from stone with roofs of different construction. The use of building materials or the choice of the shape of the roof had obviously nothing to do with chronological development, but was influenced by the amount and the type of material that it was possible to obtain.

The other inhumations were in simple grave pits, oblong in shape, which were usually not constructed in any special way. Only in rare cases did one find that the sides or the floor of the pit were of unusual construction. In inhumation 51 the floor of the grave was hollowed out in the middle so that along the long sides were formed steps raised 10 cm above the bottom. The design of grave 52 was more complicated: two steps of heights 40 and 30 cm were dug above the floor along the long sides of the grave, and near the south side was a third step 20 cm high. The steps were comparatively narrow (6-8 cm wide) and were probably covered by wood to a height of 40 cm, thus forming the grave.

The floors of some of the graves were hollowed out like a dish so that the head and the feet lay higher than the body (inhumations 66, 67 and 103). In inhumation 85 the head was placed higher than the body. The trough-like hollowed out floor of grave 9 was covered by a dark layer which was probably the remains of a bed of some organic matter on which the body had been placed.

No trace of wood survived in the sandy soil, and so there was no proof that wooden coffins were used, but there were some indications that they had been present in some graves. In grave 145 there was dark soil under and beside the skeleton, probably the remains of wood. Around the skeleton there were large iron nails with their points towards the body and in this way they marked the outline of the coffin. There were 3 large nails near the feet, which were slightly raised, perhaps from the lid of the coffin. E. Vágo mentions similarly placed nails in an inhumation in the cemetery at Bölcske and also traces of a wooden coffin.[84] In grave 58 there were 2 nails near the head and one near the feet. In grave 139 there was a large nail behind the head and a second by the feet but there were no traces of wood. In inhumation 28 there was an iron clinch behind the head and another near the heels. Judging by the location of the nails in these inhumations one can assume that they came from coffins. There were dark strips around the skeleton in grave 142, most probably remains of wood. Judging by the placing of the grave-goods in the graves there were no wooden coffins in the other inhumations.

In grave 55 there were fragments of bricks above the head of the skeleton and also on its feet. The skeleton was disturbed with the skull upside down and the chest damaged, but the grave-goods remained in their place. These circumstances indicate that the disturbance might have had some ritual significance. There were 3 large stones above the skeleton in inhumation 82, but it was not usual to find stones in the inhumations. The placing of stones immediately above the body does not necessarily indicate a surface structure; the possibility cannot be excluded that this was the case as in this inhumation.

We may divide the graves into two main groups according to their depth. The first group consists of shallow pits 45-95 cm deep. These inhumations were often damaged by ploughing or by the digging of holes for trees. Inhumations of the second group were 100-200 cm deep. The average depth of the deep inhumations was 100-145 cm, the deepest pits being 150-200 cm (found in only 9 inhumations). Among these were the inhumations of men with bronze brooches (burials 7, 10, and 84) and richly furnished burials of women (nos. 3 and 41). We are of the opinion, however, that the actual depth of the grave below the modern surface depended on changes in the surface levels in post-

Roman times. The depth of the grave had nothing to do with the importance of the person buried: we base this statement on the fact that in half of the deep inhumations there were no grave-goods or else they contained only poor finds (graves 33, 44, 46 and 48). The measurements of the graves of both these groups were more or less the same; the average length was 180-210 cm and the width 60-75 cm. In the smaller inhumations (120-150 cm long) were buried children and young people (graves 23, 31, 34 and 85). In the other graves 160-175 cm long were women's skeletons or those that were flexed (graves 22, 35 and 83). It is interesting to note that the extraordinary long graves 140 (235 cm) and 144 (250 cm) had unusual orientations (north-south, and south-west - north-east). Grave 47 cut into grave 42 and consequently the pit was enlarged. Roughly two thirds of the inhumations in the cemetery were deep graves of the second type, and that is why they yielded very rich grave-goods.

The orientation of the skeletons was in two basic directions. 31 skeletons (about 50% of the total) lay with their heads to the north-west. 21 skeletons (30%) lay the other way round, with their heads to the south-east. We noted deviations from this main axis only in a few cases. Five skeletons were lying with their heads west or south-west·so that more than half of the total lay with their heads to the west. Five were buried with their heads to the north, three to the north-east and two to the south.

In a few instances one inhumation was superimposed upon another. Grave 20 lay above the south-east part of grave 19; between them was a layer of sand 12 cm thick. Grave 20 was dated to the middle of the 4th century by a brooch of the onion type. In grave 19 there was deposited a typical grave group of the 2nd century: a yellow fabric jug and medium sized grey cup; there was also a small burnished dish on a foot-ring of a type used in the middle of the 4th century. From the pots found in grave 19 it is possible to date it to the first half of the 4th century. The time difference between graves 19 and 20 was only about 30-40 years.

The south-eastern part of burial 47 cut into the north-west part of no. 42. The skeleton in grave 42 was piled up in a heap and the pots were in situ; a grey jug with spout and a small dish which is a typical grave-group for inhumations of the 4th century. In grave 47 there was found a group of vessels used in burials, namely a yellow jug and a small grey pot; there was also a small red jug. The quoted instances go to show that the use of the yellow jug with the small grey pot carried on and that their use did not stop in the 2nd century.

Burial 62 was also disturbed by a later inhumation, no. 63, so that only the lower extremities remained in situ. Nothing was found in the lower inhumation. The finds in grave 63 dated from the 4th century: a small grey dish and iron rivets from footwear. Grave 83 was situated across the feet of the skeleton in grave 82, and was disturbed by the later burial. A grey jug with spout typical of the 4th century was found in burial 82, and burial 83 did not yield any finds.

Inhumations 147-148 can be considered as a double inhumation since the skeletons lay parallel and there was one single dark fill in which the outlines of separate graves could not be distinguished. The lower skeleton (no. 148) was at a depth of 105 cm, and skeleton 147 lay above it in a bent position at a depth of 90 cm so that the upper part of the body of 147 was resting on the legs of skeleton 148. From this it was obvious that skeleton 148 was buried earlier than skeleton 147, though it was not possible to date the double inhumations 147-148 as there were no associated finds except an animal bone lying beside the leg of skeleton 148.

In some instances inhumations disturbed earlier burials, the contents of which got into their fills. The fill of grave 66 was dark earth in which there were cremated bones, and sherds and a lamp. In inhumation 103, probably of the 4th century by the onion-shaped brooch which was found in it, there were found, immediately above the skeleton, the remains of a cremation (fragments of burned bones, fused glass, potsherds and a lamp). Grave 140 was filled with dark earth which contained small fragments of burned bones from a cremation, which were also among the earth fill of grave 142. Sherds of terra sigillata in the fill of grave 7 probably came from an earlier burial.

In inhumations at Rusovce the body usually lay on its back in an extended position. This position was found in 44 inhumations. In some instances the skeleton lay on its right side with the legs retracted, and these burials did not have the usual orientation north-west. In graves 22, 83 and 147 the head of the skeleton pointed south-east, in no. 28 the head pointed north, and in no. 57 south. In burial 62 only the lower extremities had survived and those were retracted, the head having probably been orientated south-east. There were no finds with the skeletons in graves 22 and 57 but judging by their situation in the cemetery they probably dated from the 4th century. No. 147, with no grave-goods, was situated among the 2nd century burials, but there was no dating evidence otherwise. A damaged middle bronze coin, a yellow jug and iron clamps were found in grave 28. Judging by the finds this burial could have dated from the 3rd century.

In grave 45 the skeleton pointed in an unusual direction (north-east - south-west); it looked as if it had been carelessly thrown there and there were no grave-goods. It is evident that an unusual posture of the skeleton was in most cases connected with a different direction. In grave 7, the skeleton of a man lay face downwards with the legs crossed. This inhumation contained the following grave-goods: a bronze brooch, a glass goblet, a small jug, a small dish containing the bones of a bird, a knife and an awl. It was therefore not the grave of a person of little social standing, thrown in carelessly, because the body was buried according to the prevailing customs with the requisite grave-goods.

When describing the position of the body in the grave the position of the arms should be noted. Most often the hands were found to be on the lap (graves 3, 4, 10, 12, 16, 23, 29, 51, 56, 84, 103 and 140), or one hand was on the lap and the other lay straight beside the body (graves 1, 14, 15, 18, 25, 30, 52, 53, 82, 83, 145 and 148). In some instances the hands were placed on the waist (graves 19, 32, 37, 66, 67, 70, 139 and 142). Other skeletons had one hand on the waist and the other on the lap (graves 9, 46, 119 and 167), only rarely were the arms stretched out alongside the body (graves 41, 58, 71 and 114). In a few cases a skeleton had its arms on its chest (grave 35) or with one arm on the chest and the other on the waist (graves 38 and 47). The legs were usually outstretched except for the mentioned instances of skeletons with retracted limbs. Only two skeletons

had their legs crossed below the knees (graves 56 and 145) and one skeleton
had its legs crossed at the knees (grave 7). In some inhumations the skeletons were completely destroyed by the action of the soil but the grave-goods
remained in their original places (graves 17, 31 and 34); in other inhumations the skeletons were preserved but there were no grave-goods (graves
33, 61 and 85): these were in most cases bodies of children or of young
persons. A number of inhumations were damaged by outside interference
and the skeletons were only partially preserved, for instance graves 26 and
135. In grave 40 only half of the skeleton survived, while in no. 42 the
bones had been deliberately piled up. In grave 44 the skeleton lay in the
corner of the grave; in no. 48 there remained only fragments of bones. The
skeleton in grave 62 was destroyed by the later inhumation no. 63; similarly in
grave 83 the skeleton was damaged by the digging of grave 82, and in grave
166 the skeleton was destroyed by a tree-hole.

In the case of inhumations the sex of the dead was not determined anatomically. Some of the inhumations were classified as male or female on the
basis of the grave-goods present, and the children's graves were identified
by their size and the length of the skeleton. Inhumations containing onion-
shaped brooches, iron rivets from footwear, iron knives and awls were regarded as those of males. We did not find any weapons in the cemetery. When
assessing the male and female bones we took the height of the skeleton and
the thickness of the bones into consideration. As typical signs of female inhumations we picked out various ornaments, e.g. necklaces, bracelets, bone
beads, combs and mirrors. In this way there were identified 23 male inhumations, namely nos 7, 9, 10, 12, 15, 18, 25, 29, 30, 32, 37, 46, 56, 58, 63,
66, 67, 84, 103, 119, 140, 144 and 167; 9 female inhumations (nos. 1, 4, 17,
21, 41, 51, 53, 70 and 142) and 5 children (nos. 23, 31, 34, 85 and 102).
Grave 35 with a brooch was probably a male one. It is also possible that
burial 3 was a male one as an iron knife and a folded beaker was found there;
however there were also bracelets and a glass bottle there. We consider the
skeletons in graves 14, 52 and 55 to have been female as they had bracelets
on their arms. From the total of 68 inhumations in simple graves, 36% were
male, 18% female and 8% children; 18% were indeterminate and contained
grave-goods and 20% were indeterminate and contained no grave-goods.

The above shows that more than 20% of the inhumations contained no grave-
goods, the rest of the graves being furnished. Among these we distinguish
items of dress (buckles, brooches, hobnails) and ornaments (bracelets, necklaces, rings) and grave-goods proper (coins, glass, pottery). Iron nails and
clamps were connected with the coffins.

Items of dress were usually on the skeleton in the same place as they were
normally worn. In the male inhumations bronze brooches of the onion type
were usually to be found on the right shoulder. The cloak was fastened on this
shoulder so that the right arm had free movement (graves 9, 10, 12, 15, 20,
25, 29, 32, 103, 144 and 166). In only one inhumation (no. 84) was the brooch
found to be on the left shoulder. It is worth noting that the men with the brooches
were buried with the heads facing north-west, save no. 32 where the head and
body pointed south-east. The skeleton in grave 35 was orientated with its head
to the south-east and had a bronze brooch near the right arm which proved that
it was originally fastened on the right shoulder. The bronze buckles were

usually found lying near the right side or near the right leg even if two buckles belonged to the same garment (burials 12, 30, 31 and 140). Only in burial 32 where the body lay with the head pointing south-east, were buckles found near the left leg. Buckles made of iron, just like those of bronze, were used for fastening belts and were usually found near the right leg (burials 18, 46, 102 and 144).

In inhumations in which the skeleton lay with the head pointing south-east there were found groups of iron hobnails near the legs. Dark patches remained in some graves, probably the remains of organic matter on which the hobnails were ranged in rows above one another. We consider these nails to be the remains of leather footwear (burials 37, 56, 58, 63, 66, 67 and 119).

There were beads from necklaces scattered around the neck and underneath the skull in the female inhumations (nos. 1, 2, 4, 17, 21, 41, 51, 70, 142), and in graves 1 and 2, more beads lay near the right shoulder. Ornamental bracelets made of bronze and bone were found on the right and left arms. There was usually one bracelet on the right arm (graves 2, 41, 52 and 55) but the skeleton in grave 14 had two. The number of bracelets on the left arm varied from one to five (graves 1, 2, 3, 14 and 41).

Rings were worn by men and women alike and were even found in a child's grave. The men had the ring usually on the right hand (burials 12 and 144), women wore rings on either hand (burials 14, 41, 53 and 142). There were two rings on either hand of the child's skeleton in grave 102.

Iron knives were found in men's graves. The knife lay in most cases near the right leg, having probably been suspended from the belt (burials 37, 46 and 102). However, the knife in grave 25 lay under a small dish, that in grave 30 was under the shin-bone together with a buckle and the one in grave 144 lay across the shin-bone together with coins. In these instances the knives were placed in the graves separately. The knives which were found near the left leg or between the legs might have been fastened to the belt (graves 40, 103, 3 and 140). In some cases the knives were placed near the right shoulder (graves 31, 32, 84, 145 and 167). In grave 31 the knife lay near the child's head together with a buckle, so a belt must have lain there originally.

The location of the coins in inhumations is important. In most cases the coins lay near the fingers at the right hand (graves 2, 3, 10, 12, 30 and 84) or at the end of the left hand (graves 11, 14, 70). One can also assume that the coins found near the pelvic bones must originally have been near the fingers of the dead person (graves 29 and 32). In some cases the coins were placed on the chest of the corpse (graves 31, 32 and 140). A considerable number of the coins were found near the right leg of the skeleton: they must have been placed into some sort of pocket (graves 9, 17, 25 and 144). In grave 41 the coins lay near the left leg and in grave 2 they were placed at the end of the legs. In only one instance (grave 28) was the coin found in the mouth. In a small number of the burials the coins lay in various places, perhaps because they had fallen from their original place, e.g. in graves 2 and 17. In burial 14 three coins lay near the right shoulder and two near the fingers of the left hand, similarly in burial 32 four coins lay on the left part of the pelvis and one on the right shoulder-blade.

Fifty-two Roman coins were found in 21 inhumations. There was no fixed number of coins which one gave to the deceased: in most cases only one coin was placed in the grave, as is borne out by 8 burials (nos. 3, 7, 10, 11, 28, 29, 70 and 84). Two coins were found in each of 5 inhumations (nos. 9, 12, 18, 31 and 41) and three coins each in graves 140 and 144. Four coins were found in 3 burials (nos. 17, 25 and 30); five coins each were in graves 14 and 32, and lastly six coins were in grave 2.

We cannot see any unified pattern in the placing of glass vessels as in nearly every grave the glass was put in a different place. In graves 9 and 102, glass beakers for drinking were near the head. Commonly they were on the right side of the body. In graves 1 and 32 the beakers were found near the right shoulder; the skeleton in grave 7 lay on its face, but had it lain on its back the beaker would also have been near the right shoulder; in graves 3, 144 and 167 the vessels were near the right elbow, in grave 103 near the right thigh, and in grave 21 by the end of the right leg. In grave 51 the beaker was at the left side of the skeleton near the thigh, in graves 12 and 53 at the end of the left leg, and between the legs in burial 30. The only small glass jug that was found lay on the right thigh bone in grave 1, and a cup in inhumation 15 was at the feet of the skeleton. Glass toilet bottles were placed in different spots: near the left leg (graves 4 and 53), between the legs (no. 3) near the right arm (no. 144), and near the left arm (no. 2). A second glass bottle in no. 2 lay in the corner of the grave.

Pots of various types and shapes were found at Rusovce in great numbers. When we examine the location of vessels in the inhumations we have to consider the types and the combinations of these types. Pots were located in the graves at various places. 75% of the vessels were found near the legs of the skeleton, 15% near the arms and 10% near the head or the trunk. The placing of the vessels near the legs can be subdivided thus: near the feet, 9 vessels; near the right foot, 10 vessels; near the left foot, 17 vessels; near the right leg, 12 vessels; near the left leg, 3 vessels; and near the knees, 2 vessels. The vessels near the arms were placed thus: near the right shoulder, 6 vessels; near the right arm, 1 vessel; near the left shoulder, 3 vessels; near the left elbow, 2 vessels. Near the head there were 3 vessels, on the chest there was one and near the pelvis there were 2 vessels.

Equally important is the question of what types of vessel were used for ritual purposes. The ones that occurred most often were sets of grey pots, consisting of a jug with spout, a jug or small jug for drinks and a flat dish with food. The set of a jug with spout and a dish was found in 5 graves (nos. 1, 7, 10, 18 and 21), the jug and dish in 2 graves (nos. 14 and 53), and a folded beaker with a dish was found in 2 graves (nos. 3 and 9). In grave 52 there was a complete set: a jug with spout, a small jug and a dish. The set of grey ceramics was found in 15 graves.

In a further 9 inhumations mixed sets were found, namely a grey vessel and one of a different fabric, for instance, a grey dish and a red jug (grave 2), a grey dish and a small colour-coated jug (grave 31), or a colour-coated dish and a grey jug (grave 25). In those burials in which there was another pottery vessel in addition to the basic ritual set, there was usually a glazed decorated vessel (graves 1, 18, 21 and 29).

With the vessels were also connected the remains of food, specifically meat, in inhumations. There were on occasions bird bones, probably chicken, on flat dishes. A small dish containing the bones of birds was found in graves 17 and 144 near the right leg, in no. 7 by the knees, and in no. 14 under the sole of the left foot. In the following burials the bird-bones were preserved without the dish and were found in various places: in graves 9 and 142 they were on the chest of the skeleton, in grave 140 near the left arm, in no. 30 in the left hand and lastly in graves 10 and 41 on the pelvis.

As was pointed out earlier, the body generally lay with the head pointing north-west. Another group consisted of those inhumations in which the body lay with the head pointing south-east. Amongst these, burial 32 contained finds which usually accompanied skeletons orientated north-west (an onion-shaped brooch, Roman coins), so that it did not belong to the inhumations of this "south-eastern" group. Some of the burials where the skeleton was pointed south-east were unfurnished (nos. 22, 61, 62, 83, 85, 147 and 148). It is interesting to note that both the double burials found in the cemetery contained skeletons with their heads pointing south-east (burials 62-63 and 147-148). Skeletons of this group were often badly preserved, their average height was 150-155 cm, and some of them, in contrast to the skeletons which were north-west orientated, had their legs crossed (nos. 22, 83 and 147). Most of the graves were 80-100 cm deep, and consequently they belonged to the group of shallow inhumations.

The inventories of these inhumations show certain peculiarities. Iron hobnails from footwear were found near the legs (burials 37, 56, 58, 63, 66, 67 and 119). The only knee-brooch was found in grave 35, which dates this inhumation to the 3rd century. Only in burials with this orientation were found the grey cups and the majority of the yellow jugs that came from 2nd century burials. Yellow jugs were also found in burials with the north-south and north-east - south-west orientation (burials 28 and 139). We consider that the different orientation of the skeleton and the characteristic grave-goods justify the classification of these inhumations as a separate group. Without further evidence it is impossible to decide whether in these were graves of a different ethnic group or whether the variation of burial rites was caused by chronological differences. It is quite possible that this group of burials dated from the 3rd century, a date which would be borne out by the brooch from grave 35.

GLASS

More glass vessels were found in the inhumations than in the cremations, though only a few complete vessels were preserved. The majority of the thin-sided beakers had been crushed by the weight of the soil. In the burials we found 24 glass vessels of various types and in 3 graves there were fragments of vessels of uncertain form. Half of the surviving vessels were drinking cups made of thin glass usually of a green colour. Here we can distinguish 3 basic types: a tall conical cup, a smaller cylindrical cup and a wider hemispherical cup. The tall conical cups were represented by 7 specimens, and were further divided into sub-groups. A completely straight-sided cup of conical shape with a straight edge was found in grave 167 (height 8 cm); the same type but with a slightly out-turned rim came from grave 102 (height 10.5 cm; fig.73, no. 6). Other conical cups (graves 103 and 144) were on small foot-rings (heights 10.5 cm, 11.5 cm: fig. 73, no. 7). Fragments of a similar cup were in grave 30 (height c. 11 cm). The cup from grave 9 differed from the previous cups by its almost cylindrically-shaped body which flowed into one with its small foot-ring, the rim being out-turned (11.5 cm; fig. 73, no. 8). The cups from graves 21 and 32 were broken and it was impossible to determine their shape more precisely. As can be seen, the tall drinking cups were all approximately 10.5-11.5 cm high. The cup from grave 53 (fig.74, no. 1) differed considerably from the undecorated cups just described. It was a conical cup on a small foot-ring with a straight rim, decorated with diagonal fluting, and it was higher than the others (14 cm).

A complete cup of the second type was found in grave 1. It was a cylindrical vessel with a straight rim and rounded bottom (height 8.2 cm; fig. 73, no. 3). The cup from grave 3 (which was reconstructed) was of the same shape (height 8.2 cm; fig. 73, no. 4). To the third type was cups of hemispherical shape. The best preserved example was from grave 15, with an out-turned rim (height 7 cm), and a similar cup came from grave 12 (height 7.7 cm; fig. 73, no. 5). We can assume that the glass fragments found in graves 7 and 51 belonged to this type of vessel.

Another common type of glass vessel was the unguentarium, of which there were some variations in shape. Two small unguentaria from grave 2 had hemispherical bodies with flattened bases, and the rim of one was widened in a funnel-like fashion (heights 8 cm and 10 cm; fig. 73, no. 1; fig. 72, no. 11). An unguentarium of similar shape came from grave 144 (height c. 7 cm). The example from grave 53 differed from these in its asymmetrically widened rim (height 8 cm; fig. 72, no. 10). The unguentarium from grave 3 had a spherical body and a slightly bent neck with a reinforced rim (height 7.5 cm; fig. 72, no. 9). This survey shows that the height of the unguentaria was 7-10 cm. Vessels of this size were used for perfumes or toilet oils. There was a slightly larger bottle from grave 4 which was broken; its lower part was conical, the base was pressed in and the rim funnel-like; as it was broken the height could not be determined exactly (approx. 11 cm). It was probably filled with oil (fig. 73, no. 2). From grave 52 came a broken bottle of which nothing remained but the neck with a turned-out rim. Judging by the fragment, this vessel was bigger than those used for oil and was probably part of a drinking set.

Other types of glass vessel were represented by single examples. A small vase with a spherical body, and a low neck with a turned-out rim made of rough green glass was preserved in grave 36 (height 3.5 cm; fig. 74, no. 2). It probably belonged to a toilet set. The most beautiful glass find from the Rusovce burials was the jug from grave 1 (fig. 74, no. 3). It was remarkable not only for its proportions but also for its decoration. The egg-shaped body was decorated with spiral trails and at the point where the body joined the neck there was a decorative collar. A similar decoration formed the rim of the jug, the foot-ring was formed by a star-shaped decoration and the elongated handle was decorated with grooves. The vessel was made of yellow glass and the decorations were in green glass (height 12 cm). The jug together with a cup formed a drinking set of high quality.

The glass vessels in the Rusovce burials can be divided into two groups according to their use: vessels for toilet purposes and those for drinking. Unguentaria for storing oil were found in burials as early as the 2nd century. That these unguentaria with their shape unaltered were used also in the 4th century was proved by the finds from the cemeteries in Pannonia. A. Radnóti writes when describing the finds in Intercisa that the unguentaria occurred in the 4th century graves. This author named these vessels 'unguentaria of the eastern type'.[85]

In Hungary drinking cups were very frequently found among the grave-goods in inhumations of the 4th century. We can see this when studying the finds from the larger sites.

A. Radnóti pointed out that at Intercisa in the inhumations of the 4th century there was a very common type of vessel, namely the conical cup which kept cropping up in many variations. Among these were slim conically shaped cups and those of almost cylindrical shape. As a second type of cup found in graves of the 4th century this author quotes as an example a hemispherical vessel. In his opinion the importing of glass from the east ended in the second half of the 3rd century. Western imports reached a peak in the first half of the 4th century. These artefacts were carried on the Danube to Pannonia mainly from the glass-manufacturing centres in the Rhineland.[86] Parallels with all the various types of tall cups from Rusovce also occur in the cemeteries at Ságvár: straight-sided cups, and cups on a short stem.[87] The cups from Ságvár were mostly made from green glass. Here we also see the parallel for the hemispherical cup from Rusovce, which shows that this type of vessel formed part of the normal furnishings of the late Roman inhumations.[88] L. Barkóczi points out that the Ságvár cemetery yielded some fine glass: various types of jugs, bottles and conical cups. According to him these types flourished in Pannonia between the years 320-375. The vessels were meticulously made from glass which was either colourless or greenish, both types having very thin walls. The quality of manufacture deteriorated in the latter part of the 4th century, the sides of the vessels becoming rough and the colour becoming green or blue.[89]

Cups similar to those from Rusovce were also found not only in Pannonia but also in the area of their manufacture. O. Doppelfeld mentions a conical cup from the collection in Cologne and dates it ito the 4th century.[90] He points out that side by side with the simple cups either with or without footrings, there were also hemispherical drinking cups. The yellow-green glass cup with decorated sides found in grave 53 at Rusovce was very similar to the vessels of the 5th century and was probably one of the earliest products of this type.

The jug with the moulded decoration from grave 1 was probably not the only example from Pannonia. Jugs of this type were also found in other cemeteries, but they were not so richly decorated. A similarly shaped jug was found at Intercisa; the body and handle were decorated by grooves, but it did have any decoration on the neck. A. Radnóti considers this type of jug to be of western type, occurring widely in Gaul and Germany.[91] A. Burger quotes jugs of this type among the finds of glass from Ságvár. These vessels were decorated with spiral trails like the Rusovce jug, but it lacked the other decoration.[92] From the examples quoted, the Rusovce jug can be considered to come from a western workshop and is typical of the 4th century.

This identification is based on glass vessels manufactured in the Rhineland quoted by O. Doppelfeld in his work. The method of decorating glass vessels with spiral trails was used from the second century, and in the 4th century more substantial moulded decorations were added.[93] According to that author there were two parallel trends: one was the increasingly widespread use of glass vessels, the other variation in quality of those vessels. There was already a great difference in the 4th century between cheap vessels designed for daily use and objets d'art made of glass.[94] The jug from grave 1 at Rusovce was in the style of the 4th century, when richly decorated vessels were very popular.

The dating of individual types of glass vessel is confirmed by Roman coins which were found in the same graves. The small unguentaria in grave 2 were accompanied by coins of Constantine I and his sons (306-350), and in grave 3 by a coin of Constantine I (306-337), which dates both burials to the 4th century. The latest coin accompanying the bottle in grave 144 was one of Constantius II (337-361), which dates the grave to the second half of the 4th century. The dating of the beakers was also based on the associated coins. The earliest form is the cylindrical cup from grave 9, dated by the coins of Galerius Maximianus (305-311) to the beginning of the 4th century. A tall conical cup from grave 30 dated, according to the associated coins of Constantius II (337-361), to the second half of the 4th century. Also dating from the second half of the 4th century was a hemispherical cup from grave 12, found with a coin of Valens (364-378). We do not know the form of the broken vessel from grave 32, but according to the coin of Valerius Severus with which it was found (305-307) it must have still have been in use at the beginning of the 4th century.

No.	Emperor	Date	Denomination	Reverse legend	No.	Mint	Cohen	Grave number
1.	Maximianus Herculius	286-305	AE2	SACR. MONET. AUGG. ET CAESS NOSTR.	1	AQS-Aquilea	VI. 504	10
2	Constantius Chlorus	292-306	AE1	GENIO POPULI ROMANI	1	P-C, or PLC-Lugdunum?	VII. 120	29
3	Valeria	292-315	AE2	VENERI VICTRICI U	1	HT Γ	VII. 2	32
4	Valerius Severus	305-307	AE2	GENIO POPULI ROMANI	1	SMSD	VII. 28	32
5	Galerius Maximianus	305-311	AE2	GENIO POPULI ROMANI	1	-QS- Aquilea	VII.87	9
6	Galerius Maximianus	305-311	AE2	SACR MONETT AUGG ET CAESS	1	Illegible	VII.188	9
7	Constantine I	306-337	AE3	(GLORIA EXERCITUS?)	1	SMA?	VII. 245	144
8	Constantine I	306-337	AE3	GLORIA EXERCITUS	1	Γ SIS - Siscia	VII. 245	14
9	Constantine I	306-337	AE3	GLORIA EXERCITUS	1	Illegible	VII. 253	14
10	Constantine I	306-337	AE3	GLORIA EXERCITUS	1	SMTSA-Thessalonica	VII.254	14
11	Constantine I	306-337	AE3	IOVI CONSERVATORI A	1	SIS-Siscia	Cohen II VI.335	17
12	Constantine I	306-337	AE3	SOLI INVICTO COMITI	1	TA	VII. 536	17
13	Constantine I	306-337	AE3	SOLI INVICTO COMITI	1		VII. 519	3
14	Constantine I	306-337	AE3	SOLI INVICTO COMITI	1		VII. 530	32
15	Constantine I	306-337	AE3	D N CONSTANTINUS MAX AUG VOT XX	1	TS Γ VI-Thessalonica	VII. 123	140
16	Constantine I	306-337	AE3	D N CONSTANTINUS MAX AUG VOT XX	1	ASIS-Siscia	VII. 123	140
17	Constantine I	306-337	AE3	--- VOT PR	1	TT-Ticinum	VII. 640	32
18	Constantine I	306-337	AE3	O: CONSTANTINOPOLIS R: without legend	1	CONOB Constantinople	VI.21	2
19	Constantine I	306-337	AE3	O: CONSTANTINOPOLIS R: without legend	1	CONS B Constantinople	VII. 21	14
20	Constantine I	306-337	AE3	O: URBS ROMA R: without legend	1	SMHA Heraclea	VII. 17	2
21	Constantine I	306-337	AE3	O: URBS ROMA R: without legend	1	Illegible	VII. 17	30
22	Constantine I	306-337	AE3	without legend	1	SMIS?	VII. 760	2
23	Helena	306-328	AE3	PAX PUBLICA?	1	Illegible	VII. 4	30
24	Licinius I	307-323	AE2	GENIO IMPERATORIS	1	TITA?	VII. 43	25
25	Licinius I	307-323	AE2	IOVI CONSERVATORI	1	SMTS-Thessalonica	VII. 78	17
26	Licinius I	307-323	AE3	IOVI CONSERVATORI	1	SIS-Siscia	VII. 67	17
27	Licinius I	307-323	AE3	IOVI CONSERVATORI A	1	SIS-Siscia	VII. 76	25
28	Licinius I	307-323	AE3	IOVI CONSERVATORI A	1	SIS-Siscia	VII. 76	25
29	Licinius I	307-323	AE3	IOVI CONSERVATORI A	1	SIS-Siscia	VII. 73	31
30	Licinius I	307-323	AE3	IOVI CONSERVATORI E	1	SIS-Siscia	VII. 86	32
31	Licinius I	307-323	AE3	IOVI CONSERVATORI E, AUGG NN	1	SIS-Siscia	VII. 67?	84
32	Licinius I	307-323	AE3	VIRTUS EXERCIT VOT XX	1	SIS-Siscia	VII. 193	25
33	Delmatius	335-337	AE3	GLORIA EXERCITUS	1	ASIS-Siscia	VII. 11	14
34	Constantine II	335-340	AE3	CLARITAS REIPUBLICAE	1	Δ SIS-Siscia	VII. 57	31
35	Constantine II	335-340	AE3	GLORIA EXERCITUS	1	SMKS-Cyzicus	VII.122	2
36	Constantine II	335-340	AE3	GLORIA EXERCITUS	1	SMNS-Nicomedia	VII. 122	2
37	Constantine II	335-340	AE3	PROVIDENTIAE CAESS	1	ESIS-Siscia	VII. 163	70
38	Constans	335-350	AE1	FEL TEMP REPARATIO	1	SIS-Siscia	VII. 22	41
39	Constans	335-350	AE3	FEL TEMP REPARATIO	1	SA	VII. 10	41
40	Constans	335-350	AE3	GLORIA EXERCITUS	1	ASIS-Siscia	VII. 48	2
41	Constans	335-350	AE3	GLORIA EXERCITUS	1	ASIS-Siscia	VII. 73	144
42	Crispus	+ 337	AE3	CAESARUM NOSTRORUM - VOT X	1	ESIS-Siscia	VII. 44	140
43	Constantius II	337-361	AE3	GLORIA EXERCITUS	1	SISC-Siscia	VII. 92	30
44	Constantius II	337-361	AE3	GLORIA EXERCITUS	1	SMTA	VII. 92	30
45	Constantius II	337-361	AE3	GLORIA EXERCITUS	1	Illegible	VII. 104	144
46	Valens	364-378	AE3	SECURITAS REIPUBLICAE	1	TIT	VIII. 47	11
47	Valens	364-378	AE3	RESTITUTOR REIPUBLICAE	1	Illegible	VIII. 31	12
48	Valens	364-378	AE3	RESTITUTOR REIPUBLICAE	1	SIS-Siscia	VIII. 31	12

COINS

52 Roman bronze coins were found in the inhumations at Rusovce. However, only 48 could be studied as two were damaged and two disintegrated during excavation.

The following coins from the third and early fourth century were found: middle bronze of Maximianus Herculius, first bronze of Constantius Chlorus, middle bronze of Galeria Valeria, middle bronze of ·Severus II and two middle bronze of Galerius Maximianus. The majority of the coins (16 small bronzes) were of Constantine I (306-337). Among them were two coins of the URBS ROMA type and two of the CONSTANTINOPOLIS type. A second large group was formed by coins of the sons of Constantine I: Crispus (1 piece), Constantine II (4 pieces) Constans (4 pieces) and Constantius II (3 pieces). Further coinage of the period of Constantine I was represented by one piece of Helena, 1 of Delmatius and 9 of Licinius I. The latest coins to be found were 3 of Valens (364-378). It is evident from the coins found in the inhumations that the burial ground at Rusovce can be roughly dated to between 290 and 380. The majority of the preserved coins had legible mint-marks so that it was possible to determine their origin. Coins from the mint of Siscia, modern Šišak in Jugoslavia, predominated - they represented 40% of all the coins (19 pieces). The other mints were represented by single pieces: Aquileia (2 pieces), Heraclea (1 piece), Constantinople (2), Cyzicus (1), Nicomedia (1), Thessalonica (3), Ticinum (1). The geographical origin of these coins reflects the prevailing trade relations and the influx of soldiers into army encampments in this part of Pannonia. *

---

*

The Roman coins were identified according to the work of H. Cohen: Description historique des monnaies frappees sous l'empire romaine, 2nd edition, Leipzig, 1930.

POTTERY

The pottery from the inhumations consisted of a greater variety of vessels and types than that from the cremations. Besides those types known from cremations (grey rough-surfaced, yellow and red colour-coated fabrics) there were further groups manufactured by a different technique (glazed ceramics, and burnished vessels). On the other hand there were no terra sigillata vessels or their imitations, or the delicate thin-walled pots. The types of fabric used in cremations were now manufactured in new forms; for example, the grey fabric with the rough surface instead of being represented only by the simple cup was represented by jugs with spouts, jugs, small jugs and dishes. The colour-coated vessels differed from the earlier products in possessing a dark-red, thickly applied colour-coat. The pottery from the inhumations can be divided into several types according to the manner of manufacture: grey with a rough surface, yellow, colour-coated, glazed, burnished and rough.

Among these types the grey vessels with the rough surface formed the largest group, 50 examples being found. Other types of pot were represented by 35 vessels. Of the earlier forms of the grey fabric, the drinking cup found in graves 19, 47 and 48 (heights 8-13.5 cm; fig. 78, no. 12) continued in use. The second form of the grey fabric to survive in unchanged form was the folded beaker (graves 3 and 9; fig. 79, no. 1). Cups corresponding in form to 2nd century folded beakers were found in both inhumations; according to their measurements they belonged to larger vessels (heights 16 cm and 18.7 cm).

The set of drinking vessels in the inhumations consisted of a tall vessel, a jug with a spout or a jug and smaller pitchers. The six grey jugs with spouts which were found in graves 41, 42, 52, 82 and 144 were of the same form, the egg-shaped body being continuous with the low foot-ring and with the conical neck from which it was divided only by a groove; the mouth was in the shape of a trefoil and formed the outlet and the strap-handle extended from the rim to the middle of the jug (fig. 79, no. 4). Also the measurements of these jugs were more or less the same; their height varied between 19 cm and 23.5 cm, the diameter of the rim was usually 9 cm, the maximum diameter was on average 15 cm and the diameter of the base was 6.5 cm. We are obviously dealing here with a standard type of vessel. As the upper part of the neck of the pot from grave 32 was broken off it was impossible to reconstruct the rim. The remains show that it was a jug with spout, not a jug. Its measurements did not differ from those of the preceding vessels (height 20 cm).

The grey jugs occurred in smaller numbers than the jug with spout. Two similar jugs came from grave 6 and from the graves damaged in 1964; they had an oval body on a low foot-ring with a narrow neck ending in a widened out rim. Both had a coarse strap-handle (fig. 79, no. 2). The jug from grave 53 had a spherical body and a wider neck, which brought it nearer to the category of pots, but it had no spout (fig. 79, no. 6). The measurements of the jugs did not vary much; they were 21-24 cm high, the diameter of the rim was 6-8 cm, the maximum diameter was 14-16 cm, and the diameter of the base was 6.8-7.5 cm. The jug with spout and jugs were consequently roughly of the same size, their volume being about 1.5 litre. The vessel with the missing neck from grave 14 probably belonged to the pots judging by the remains of the narrow neck.

In the cremations, a small cup was used for drinking; in the inhumation this was replaced by a small jug with a handle. Altogether 12 small grey jugs of a single type were found in the inhumations at Rusovce. The small jug usually had spherical body which merged with a low foot-ring and a short neck which ended in a funnel-like widened rim; there was a rounded strap handle which usually extended to the middle of the vessel (graves 1, 7, 10, 25, 84 and 142; fig. 78, nos. 8, 10). Some of the jugs had a more pear-shaped body (graves 18, 21, 36 and 52). The small jug from grave 8 was bi-conical (fig. 78, no. 7). Although the smallest jug from grave 4 differed from other examples in having a higher foot-ring and a biconical body, we can still include it in this group (fig. 78, no. 9). The height of these jugs varied from 10 cm to 15.5 cm, the rim diameter was 6-9.5 cm, the maximum diameter was 9-13.5 cm and the foot ring was 3.7-6.5 cm. in diameter. Two more jugs of this shape were found in the cemetery. In grave 27 there were frag-ments which were reconstructed to form a small jug with a spherical body of normal size, in a yellow-grey fabric. Burial 27 was disturbed; as the frag-ments of the earlier and later pots were mixed up we do not know whether this jug belonged to the grave or not. In grave 140 there was a small jug of similar shape which did not however have any connection with the group of vessels with the rough surface. The small jug, yellow-grey in colour, had a smooth surface (height 15 cm). It differed also in that its rim was decora-ted with grooves. The find from grave 140 proves that this form was associa-ted with a group of polished vessels which we describe below.

The small, flat, plain grey dishes with straight, sloping sides and inturned rims occurred in the greatest numbers in inhumation burials (19 specimens in all). These dishes varied in size but their shape did not alter (graves 1, 2, 3, 7, 9, 10, 18, 21, 29, 31, 32, 42, 52, 53, 63, 70, 140 and 144; fig. 78, nos. 13, 15-17). Their height was 3-5.5 cm, the rim diameter varied from 15 to 21 cm, and the diameter of the base was 7.8-15.5 cm. The dish from grave 52 was asymmetrical: it was probably hand-made or badly fired. The colour of the clay of these dishes varied from light-grey to dark grey or black.

In addition to the group of grey dishes, there was also a small, deep sloping-sided carinated bowl with a decorated horizontal rim (grave 56; fig. 78, no. 14). In the inhumation burials there were also tall jugs of yellow fabric, made of alluvial clay. These jugs occurred extensively in earlier cremations, six examples were found in the inhumations: (nos. 19, 28, 37, 47, 56 and 139; fig. 80, nos. 4, 5). These jugs had the same shape and dimensions as the vessels described from cremations (height 22-29 cm). Obviously the shape of the vessel corresponded to its purpose, the storage of beverages, and it continued to be manufactured unchanged.

The colour-coated pots were made from the same yellow alluvial clay as the tall jugs. Individual vessels which were preserved at Rusovce indicate

41

the variety of forms of this ornamental type. There was a single example of a globular pot with a foot-ring and a short neck from grave 71, its entire surface covered in stripes of red colour-coat (height 13.6 cm; fig. 80, no. 11). The spherical body of the vessel merged with the foot-ring and the short neck was decorated with a band of red paint. Two sloping-sided dishes from graves 17 and 25 were colour-coated red on the inside and on the outside had a red band round the rim (rim diameters of both c. 20 cm; fig. 79, no. 10).

The above vessels were decorated in a clear red colour; the ones that follow were covered in a thick, dark red colour-coat. The small drinking cups from graves 29 and 70 were colour-coated red on the outside except for the foot-ring (fig. 81, nos. 2, 3). They were of similar shape (a globular body on a narrow foot-ring) and size (height c. 10 cm). A pear-shaped jug with a straight neck and narrow foot-ring came from grave 31; the upper part of this vessel was red colour-coated (fig. 80, no. 10). Another example from grave 1 was a small pear-shaped vessel, the body of which merged with the neck and a narrow foot-ring. It was entirely colour-coated in red (fig. 80, no. 9).

We also include among the colour-coated vessels a jug of distinctive profile from grave 55, although it was made of clay of a predominantly grey colour (fig. 81, no. 1). Its globular body was very sharply separated from an out-splayed foot-ring, the narrow neck ending in a funnel-like rim. Round the neck was an applied moulded strip. The jug had a thin red colour-coat (height 24 cm). Nine painted vessels were recovered from the inhumations at Rusovce and they can be divided into 7 different types.

We can date a larger proportion of the red colour-coated vessels because of the coins that were found with them. The cup on a foot-ring from grave 29 was deposited around the year 310, the dish from grave 25 can be dated to about 325. A second cup from grave 70, a small jug from grave 31, and a dish from grave 17 all belonged to c. 340. All the specimens of colour-coated pots which it was possible to date came from the first half of the 4th century.

From their manufacturing process, vessels made of red clay were closely connected with the yellow fabric vessels described above. They were also made of alluvial clay and were well fired. However, the vessels were of different forms from the yellow jugs. The characteristics of the jug from grave 2 were a pear-shaped body merging with a conical neck, a flat and separated foot-ring and the strap handle which extended to the girth of the vessel. It differed from the yellow jugs in its ornamentation of an applied strip on the neck and grooves on the body (fig. 80, no. 3). The jug from grave 63 was of a different shape; it had an oval body on a foot-ring and a short wide neck. The handle, which was placed on the body rather than under the rim, was singular, differing from the other vessels (height 15 cm). From grave 15 there came a small red pot with an oval body and a narrow neck ending in mouth with a spout (height 15 cm; fig. 80, no. 6). The second pot from grave 47 had a globular body and a narrow neck (height 14 cm; fig. 80, no. 7).

The burnished grey vessels were late, and were represented in the inhumations by several types: jugs, dishes and cups. The grey burnished jug from grave 17 represented a new type of tall vessel. It had a globular body on a short foot-ring, a short straight neck, and the strap handle projected above the rim (fig. 79, no. 7). The jug from grave 102 (fig. 79, no. 9) differed in shape from the grey pots with a rough surface. The pear-shaped body merged with a short foot-ring and a conical neck and the rounded handle reached to the middle of the vessel. The most important feature was its decoration of vertical bands extending over the whole body. This ornamentation was common on vessels of the 5th century. There were no other dateable grave-goods in grave 102 but from its location in the cemetery the inhumation belongs to the 4th century like the rest of the inhumations.

In graves 14 and 30 there were burnished dishes with sloping sides with in-turned rims (heights both 4.5 cm; diameters 16.5 cm, 17 cm; fig. 79 no. 8; fig. 80, no. 1). They were decorated in different ways; the first had lines and the other one had a rough band under the rim. A simple sloping-sided dish from grave 68 was undecorated. The dish from grave 19 was on a low foot-ring, and copied the terra sigillata form Dragendorff 27. (fig. 80, no. 2). Some of the burnished dishes are dated by coins: the jug from grave 17 and the small dish from grave 14 dated from c. 340; the dish from grave 30 came from c. 360.

Only those vessels which were covered with shiny yellow, green or brown burnishing belonged to the 4th century. The metallic, so-called "leaden-glaze" was typically late. There were 9 specimens of glazed vessels from the the inhumations at Rusovce and every vessel was a different type.

The most important find from the Rusovce cemetery was an anthropomorphic jug representing a female figure in a long dress, from grave 18 (fig. 81, no. 4). It was covered with a brown glaze and had dark vertical stripes. The handle had been broken in antiquity. The neck of the jug was in the form of a woman's head and neck, the long dress was represented by an oval body on a low foot-ring. The treatment of the head was as follows: the nose and chin were modelled from the fabric of the head, and the eyes and ears were applied. An incised head-gear formed the rim of the jug. The shoulders were shaped like a short bodice with a collar which formed the division from the main body of the jug, which was the long skirt. The short sleeves were moulded, the arms are rested on the stomach, and an oval cup was held in the right hand. The figure measured 29 cm in height.

This anthropomorphic vessel from Rusovce has a very close analogue in a vessel found in the Györ cemetery.[95] This is a jug with a handle, representing a female figure in a dress with a head-band and necklace; there are only small differences in the dress compared with the Rusovce example. The chief difference is in that the woman of the Györ jug, besides holding a cup in her right hand, also holds a spindle and yarn in her left hand. The following Latin inscription is engraved on the vessel: IENVARIE PIE ZESES.

E. Thomas[96] has discussed the anthropomorphic jug from Györ. The spindle and cup indicated, according to her, that the figure is the goddess of fate, Clotho, spinning the thread of life. The author studied the popularity of the cult of Clotho and came to the conclusion that it was not indigenous to Pannonia, and attributed the jug to the presence of somebody from Italy or from the Eastern Provinces. From the shape and the glaze, Thomas judged it to be the product of a pottery in Pannonia and dated it to 350-370.

On Roman sites in Pannonia there occurred anthropomorphic vessels in the shape of a human head (Kopfurnen) or smaller cups with a plastic face. F. Fülep notes that the face-vessels were popular in Roman times and were not suitable for dating. He describes a small vessel with a face from a cremation in Vasas dated to the middle of the 1st century. He quotes another vessel with a face which probably originated in the district of Baranya and also mentions a similar example found at Intercisa.[97] K. Póczy writes that the face-urns were inherited from Hellenistic traditions and occurred throughout the Roman period. A red-painted face-vessel from Intercisa dated from the time of the Severan dynasty (first third of the 3rd century). A similar vessel from Brigetio was found together with a coin of Gordian (238-244).[98] E. Thomas mentions a cup with a face which was found in the Roman villa in Tác (Gorsium). In Aquincum a cup was found with two faces (the head of Janus).[99]

All these vessels have one common feature, namely that the faces are grotesque with disproportionately large ears and a large nose (Vasas, Taqua). On a vessel from Tác the eyes were applied in the same manner as on the vessel from Rusovce. A. Schörgendorfer mentions six such vessels with faces from the Eastern Alps, from the approximate area of Noricum.[100] According to him the anthropomorphic vessels evolved from face-urns which had their origin in the Northern Iron Age. The author quotes two vessels in the shape of a woman; these however have a different stance and different costume from the ones on the vessels from Pannonia. A. Schörgendorfer thinks that the women depicted on the vessels were dressed in local styles.

The problem of anthropomorphic vessels has often attracted the attention of scholars, not only archaeologists but also art historians. Discussing the origin of urns with faces, J. Květ draws our attention to the fact that these vessels kept their basic shape and that there was only a rough outline of the human figure. According to him the anthopomorphic vessels with the naturalistic shape not only fulfilled certain conditions of the cult but also fulfilled their function.[101] This can be said of the vessel from Rusovce, which kept the shape of a jug and in all probability also fulfilled its function. J. Květ writes that the development of naturalistic anthropomorphic and zoomorphic vessels in Roman times was connected with glass manufacture. Glass cups with the face of Janus or in the shape of a human head were being manufactured in the second century in the workshops in Campania, and later on in the workshops of the Rhineland and in Gaul.[102]

The question of the dress on the vessels from Rusovce and Györ is worth mentioning. The woman's dress was modelled in high relief and was obviously taken from life. The dress consisted of a short bodice with a big round décolleté and short sleeves, and a long wide skirt. It was not a dress currently worn by Roman women at that time. Roman women wore a long loose tunic over which they wore a shorter stole. They wore different hairstyles according to the current fashion but they did not adorn their heads with high bands worn on their foreheads. We assume that the dress was connected with one of the groups of the local inhabitants. As already mentioned the women on the anthropomorphic vessel from Noricum were dressed in local styles.

The anthropomorphic vessels from Rusovce and Győr were manufactured in the same way, their size and artistic conception was the same, and there is no doubt that they were products of the same hand. This is borne out by their localised distribution: such vessels were not found on other burial places in Pannonia. The discovery of figured jugs at Rusovce and Győr (a comparatively near location) proves that in this part of Pannonia there lived a section of the population different from the people around them and that they kept up the cult of the Graeco-Roman mythology.

As another remarkable form we should mention an ornamental vase with plastic decoration and a shiny brown glaze from grave 29. The oval body of the vessel on a low foot-ring merged into a conical neck with a reinforced rim. On the body were applied alternately vertical lines of horse-shoe shaped decorations and drops en barbotine (height 21.3 cm). We do not find this form among the other types of vessel (fig. 81, no. 5).

All the remaining vessels were without moulded decoration. The small vase from grave 55 also had an oval body on a low foot-ring, a narrow neck and a yellow glaze (height 11.7 cm; fig. 81, no. 6). The second vase, from grave 102, had a yellow-green glaze on a globular body with a foot-ring and a wider straight neck with a widened rim (height 11.2 cm; fig. 81, no. 7). In grave 1 was found an amphora with three handles covered with a yellow-green glaze. The bulbous body on a narrow foot merged with a straight neck decorated with grooves and the strap handles were also decorated with grooves (height 9.5 cm; fig. 81, no. 9). The jug with a spout which we encountered in grey fabric survived and now appeared in the glazed fabric. The jug from grave 167 had a pear-shaped body on a low foot, the body merging into a straight neck ending in a spout (fig. 81, no. 11); the vessel was covered with brown glaze (height 15 cm). From grave 21 came a small jug with a yellow-brown glaze; it had an oval body on a foot, and a narrow neck with a funnel-like mouth; the strap shaped handle was folded at the bottom end into a roll-like ornament (height 14 cm; fig. 81, no. 12). The cup with two handles from grave no. 11 was an interesting shape: the cylindrical body on a narrow foot was decorated with rows of vertical grooves and covered in a green glaze (height 7.5 cm; fig. 81, no. 10). The last glazed vessel, from grave 36, was a simple cylindrical cup with a thickened rim; the brown glaze had mostly fallen off (height 6 cm; fig. 81, no. 8).

The amphora with handles from grave 1 and the cup with handles from grave 11 were made of red clay; both had an engraved decoration and possessed a similar yellow-green glaze except for the stem which was unglazed. In view of these common characteristics we can assume that these two vessels came from the same workshop. It is possible to date individual glazed vessels more accurately by the coins that were found in the graves. The decorated vase with the grave 29 dated from the beginning of the 4th century, c. 310; the cup with handles from grave 11 dated from the end of the 4th century, c. 380.

The coarse pots for daily use were put into inhumations only in small numbers. The most important was the pot from grave 4 (fig. 81, no. 13). The top third of the brown vessel was the most convex, the horizontal rim was turned outward, and its surface was decorated with shallow horizontal

45

grooves. This pot represents the prototype of Slavonic vessels of the Danubian type. J. Eisner searched for the origin of the Danubian pottery among the late Roman pots. This similarity is reinforced by a pattern on the base in the form of an irregular star (height 12.2 cm).

A greyish-yellow jug from the 1964 excavations also belongs to the coarse pottery. It has a biconical body with a narrow neck ending in a spout and a round handle (fig. 81, no. 14). It had thick walls and an uneven surface. In the disturbed grave 8 was preserved a simple purple dish and a yellow-grey pot whose globular body merged with its low foot and its funnel-like neck. One has to also include in this group the heavy vessel from grave 11: the globular body on a narrow foot merging into a funnel-like neck was decorated with vertical rows of dots which had been impressed with a pointed instrument (fig. 79, no. 3). Although the vessel was dark-grey it did not belong to the grey ceramics with a coarse surface described above, as it was not of a suitably high standard of workmanship.

The dating of the various types of pottery from the inhumations at Rusovce is made possible by the finds made on other Roman sites in Hungary. Concentrating on the numerically largest group, that of the grey vessels with the coarse surface. Surveying the late Roman domestic pottery from Intercisa, K. Póczy points out that in the second half of the 3rd century there is a decline in the quality of pottery; the forms become simpler and the vessels lose their balanced proportions. It is mainly the pottery from Intercisa which offers parallels to the vessels from Rusovce cemetery. The grey beakers that were found in the inhumations at Rusovce were also present at Intercisa. According to K. Póczy this shape was used in Pannonia until the end of the 4th century.[103] Also the folded beakers in Pannonia were used to the end of the Roman period. Parallels with the beakers from Rusovce were among the finds from Intercisa and Brigetio. These vessels in either grey or black fabric were larger and coarser.[104]

The grey jugs with spouts were produced in Pannonia in various modifications. The jugs from Rusovce were mostly similar to the Type 87 jugs from Intercisa. K. Póczy deduces that this form survived longest in the provinces of Pannonia and Noricum where it lasted to the end of the Roman period.[105] A. Schörgendorfer depicts a grey jug of similar shape.[106] E. Bónis places similar jugs with spouts among the early Roman forms when made of yellow or red clay.[107]

There are parallels for the grey jugs from Rusovce among the pottery from Intercisa.[108] These simple jugs were also made from yellow alluvial clay.

A comparatively large number of grey small jugs were found in inhumations at Rusovce. K. Póczy describes these small jugs as characteristic household vessels of the 4th century. The author notes that small jugs with handles which project above the rim occur in Pannonia exclusively in the 4th century. The popularity of these small jugs was confined to Pannonia. Besides Intercisa, K. Póczy mentions further finding places, namely Pécs, Györ, and Brigetio. and Brigetio.[109] Similar small jugs were found in the cemetery in Ságvár. A. Schörgendorfer mentions small jugs of this type from Austria and dates them to the 4th century and the first half of the 5th century.[110] The grey dishes were present at Rusovce in great numbers. It was the most popular

46

form during the whole Roman period from the 1st to the 4th century. K. Póczy writes that the small sloping-sided dishes occur throughout Pannonia (e.g. at Intercisa and Brigetio) in the 4th century. K. Burger[111] draws attention to the fact that this shape was absent only in the cemetery at Ságvár. A small bowl with a horizontal rim was found on other sites in Pannonia. K. Póczy noted that these small bowls were found at Intercisa and Aquincum.[112]

It can be seen from the analysis of the grey vessels that the forms found at Rusovce were common throughout Pannonia and its neighbourhood. These vessels are dated to the 4th century.

Painted or colour-coated vessels occurred on sites in Pannonia in several forms with the painting mostly in red. The red-painted amphora with three handles from grave 34 has parallels in the Pannonian pottery. K. Póczy mentions a similar small amphora with coloured red from Intercisa. The author mentions that amphorae with 2 or 3 handles were popular from the 1st to the 3rd centuries. A. Schörgendorfer depicts an amphora of this shape but does not describe the colour-coating. He dates this type of amphora as 2nd to 3rd century.[113]

Among the pottery described by A. Schörgendorfer there were cups on a low foot similar in shape to the ones from graves 29 and 70 at Rusovce. The author dates this form to the 4th century.[114] We find close analogies with a jug from grave 55, showing a clear division between fot and body, at Intercisa. K. Póczy looked for prototypes of these forms among metal vessels. She considered the red colour-coating on the jugs to be a glaze but mentioned that the 'glaze' was so thin that it is hard to distinguish it from the colour of the material. This type of jug occurred in the inhumations at Ságvár. A. Burger lists it among the types of domestic pottery and also considers it to be a copy of metal vessels.[115]

K. Póczy isolated from the domestic pottery at Intercisa a special group of vessels with a brown burnished surface. The author dates a small bowl. similar to the one on a stem from Rusovce, grave 19, as 4th century, although E. Bónis lists this type of small bowl among the early glazed vessels.[116] K. Póczy considers the burnished vessels to be late Roman. To this group belonged jugs decorated with vertical bands or a latticed design and dishes with sloping sides. The jug with the burnished ornamentation from Rusovce was of the same form and dimensions as a jug of this type from Intercisa.[117] Vessels with burnished decoration were found at Intercisa in inhumations which did not contain any coins. Inhumations containing these vessels were in a part of the burial ground which produced coins dating from 340-380.

The great variety of forms of this type can be seen from the survey of the glazed vessels. We find analogies with some of the forms from Rusovce among the glazed pottery from Intercisa which was studied by K. Póczy. The vessel from Intercisa had a similar shape to that from grave 29; it too was decorated with rows of applique horseshoe-like ornamentation; the difference lay only in the placing of the decoration and in the yellow colour of the glaze. A globular vase from a 4th century burial ground in Budapest (ul. Bogdani)[118] was likewise decorated with appliqué horseshoe-like ornamentation. The cup with two handles from grave 11 was similar to one from Intercisa. It was made of red clay, covered with a yellow-green glaze and with an engraved decoration. According to K. Póczy this form was widely distributed in Pannonia where it continued until the end of the 4th century. Besides the find from Intercisa the author mentions one from Brigetio.[119] A. Schörgendorfer describes this type of cup with handles, decorated with incisions and with a yellow glaze, and dates it to the second half of the 4th century.[120]

The glazed amphora with three handles can be compared with a vessel with a green-brown glaze from Ságvár. Also A. Schörgendorfer depicts a vessel of a similar shape glazed in yellow and dates it to the 4th century.[121] Glazed jugs similar to the one from Grave 167 at Rusovce were found in the Ságvár cemetery.[122] K. Póczy writes that the jugs formed the greatest part part of the glazed vessels at Intercisa. She dates the native late Roman pots as 4th century. In the Ságvár cemetery the glazed pottery is dated by the coins to 346-360.[123]

As can be seen from this survey, vessels of varying types from Rusovce cemetery had numerous parallels on other burial and dwelling sites of the Roman period in Pannonia. The spread of similar types of pottery over a wide area indicates that these were locally-produced articles and not imports. In the earlier period we noted in burials vessels imported from the west (terra sigillata, fine pottery). We do not find vessels in inhumations that stand out as being of foreign manufacture.

Pottery was manufactured in Pannonia in many places and we can assume that there were also factories in the neighbourhood of Gerulata, although we have not been able to locate them so far. We know, however, about potteries in other places. There was one in Tác (Gorsium), where glazed vessels were made. Work went on in this workshop from the end of the 3rd to the beginning of the 4th century.[124] Vessels were made in this workshop which were decorated with plastic horseshoe-shaped ornamentation. In connection with the pottery found at Intercisa, K. Póczy writes that the greatest part of vessels of a variety of forms were made in local workshops. The author followed up the distribution of the individual types of vessel and came to this conclusion: for the neighbourhood of Savaria a group of glazed vessels was characteristic, among which were jugs with spout covered with a shiny brown glaze and small vases with a yellow glaze. Tall jugs with a red colour-coat and a narrow appliqué strip on the neck were made in a workshop near Arrabona. Not far from Aquincum, globular and biconical jugs and small dishes with splayed rims were a common local type. The characteristic of the pottery in the region of Intercisa was a typical porous glaze either of green or yellow-green colour.[125] K. Póczy dates the development of the pottery manufacture in Intercisa to the end of the 3rd and the beginning of the 4th century. During this time the local workshops supplied the surrounding settlements with their products.[126]

Publication of a full and detailed study of the pottery from Rusovce and the surrounding Roman centres (Magyaróvár and Györ) will, no doubt, show the distribution of the individual types of vessels and enable us to locate their centres of manufacture.

BROOCHES

All the bronze brooches that were found in inhumations at Rusovce, except for one, belonged to the onion-shaped type, fourteen of which were found. Among these we can distinguish the 3 following types:

1. Simple, fairly small brooches (length 6.3-7.5 cm) with 3 onion-shaped knobs. The flat bow and the cross-bar were undecorated, the three knobs were divided from the cross-bar by smooth rings, the rectangular foot (vertical bar) was undecorated or was decorated only at the end by incisions, and the pin was made of bronze (graves 9, 10 and 32; fig. 82, nos. 1, 2, 3). The brooch in grave 10 was found with a coin of Maximianus Herculius (286-305); in grave 9 was a coin of Galerius Maximianus (305-311); and in grave 32 there were coins of Constantine I (306-337).

2. The brooches from graves 25, 29 and 84 can be regarded as a transitional type which combined the typical elements of types 1 and 3 (fig. 82, nos. 4, 5; 83, no. 1). The brooches were of varying lengths (6.5-8.6 cm) and had 2 or 3 onion-shaped knobs. Only on the brooch from grave 25 was the flat bow decorated. The straight cross-bar on the brooches from graves 29 and 84 had moulded decoration. On the brooch from grave 29 there were ornamental rings set between the knob and the cross-bar. The rectangular foot-plate was decorated with incisions but on the brooch from grave 29 there were indentations instead. The brooch from grave 84 had an iron pin. In grave 29 was found, together with the brooch, a coin of Constantius Chlorus (292-306); in grave 25 25 there were found coins of Licinius Sen. (307-323).

3. This group was represented by decorated brooches of various lengths (6.4-9.7 cm) with 2 or 3 onion-shaped knobs (graves 7, 12, 15, 20, 103, 144 and 167, disturbed grave fig. 83, nos. 2-4; fig. 84, nos. 1-5). This was by far the biggest group and it contained more than half of the brooches found. In grave 15 the brooch had a rather wide, arched bow with an incised decoration. The cross-bar of trapezoidal shape usually had an incised decoration, and on some brooches was perforated (graves 103 and 144). The knobs were onion-shaped, consisting of a ball with a pointed protrusion. The knobs were separated by smooth or serrated rings (graves 12, 103 and 144). The vertical rectangular bar was either decorated throughout (graves 15, 20, 103 and 144) or only on the foot-plate (graves 7, 12 and 167). The vertical bars were decorated either by incisions or by engraved rings (graves 12, 15 and 167) and by small indentations (graves 7 and 144). The brooch in grave 144 was found with coins of Constantius II (337-361), the largest brooch in grave 12 was found with coins of Valens (364-378) and the brooch from grave 7 was found with a damaged small bronze of the 4th century.

The brooches described above mostly had bronze pins, except for those from graves 12, 15 and 167 with iron pins. The brooch from grave 12 had a device for securing the pin. The brooch from grave 103 had a similar device, and a remnant of another survived on a brooch from grave 84. It is worth noting that iron pins with these guards were mostly found on brooches that were richly decorated. All the brooches described were cast; they were 2.3-3.4 cm long and 6.3-9.7 cm long, with an average length of 6.7-7.5 cm. The decoration on the bow and on the horizontal and vertical bars was composed of several elements: engraved lines, spirals, rings, concentric rings, deep incisions and small indentations. The rectangular vertical plate often had serrated edges.

The coins found with the brooches show that the three types of brooch represent a chronological development. The coins indicate that type (1), the smaller, undecorated brooches, date from the first third of the 4th century. A very modestly decorated type of brooch was also in use in the same period. The third group, the richly decorated brooches, belongs to the last two thirds of the 4th century.

V. Sakář made a survey of onion-shaped brooches found in Central Europe and he dates the ones found in Bohemia, Moravia and Slovakia to the second half of the 4th century. He assumes that the older type of onion-shaped brooch found its way on to the present-day territory of Czechoslovakia from Noricum.[127] B. Svoboda also dates the onion-shaped brooches to the 4th century. He also claims that during its development the vertical plate of the brooch became longer to afford space for the decoration.[128] A considerable number of onion-shaped brooches were found in inhumations in Pannonian cemeteries of the Roman period. In discussing the Roman cemeteries at Intercisa, K. Sági quotes finds of onion-shaped brooches in inhumations and dates them to the second half, or to the end, of the 4th century.[129] Onion-shaped brooches were found in the cemetery at Keszthelyi, where they were dated by Roman coins from Constantine I to Valens. A. Sági states that the brooches were worn on the right shoulder fastened with the vertical bar uppermost.[130] This bears out observations made at Rusovce. The onion-shaped brooches were part of a soldier's dress, and only rarely were they found in female inhumations. Brooches of this type which were found in the cemetery at Ercsi were dated by coins of Constantius II and Vetranio.[131] Forty-one onion-shaped brooches were found in the late Roman cemetery at Ságvár; some of them were of similar form and were decorated in a similar way to the brooches found at Rusovce, which others differed in being shorter and more massive.[132]

N. Beljajev has studied Byzantine brooches and in this connection he has followed up the development of the onion-shaped brooches. An older type dating from the end of the 3rd century and from the beginning of the 4th century had an undecorated horizontal bar, the spherical knobs were of the same diameter as the cross bar, the bow and the plate were decorated with incisions or with imitation filigree work. In the next group the horizontal bar became wider, but the general charcater of the brooch remained the same, and the knobs became more pointed as a transition towards the onion-shape. The third group, dating from the end of the 4th and the beginning of the 5th century, was characterised by its more elaborate decoration, the bow and plate being decorated with wavy lines and spirals, and the knobs being onion-shaped. To this group belongs also the safety device guarding the pin.

Coins of Constantine I and Gratian dated these brooches.[133]   According to
N. Beljajev the development of the onion-shaped brooches coincided roughly
with the development of the decorated brooches at Rusovce.

   Besides the onion-shaped brooches, there was found at Rusovce in grave 35
a bronze brooch of a different type. It was a smaller knee-shaped fibula with
a high fastening. M. Lámiova-Schmiedlová dates this type of brooch to the 2nd/
3rd century. The brooch from Rusovce probably belonged to the 3rd century;
it was therefore the earliest type of brooch found in an inhumation (fig. 82, no.
6).134

ORNAMENTS

Beads from necklaces were found in female inhumations, mostly made of coloured glass or glass paste. It was less usual to find beads made of gold, tin, amber or bone. Persons buried in 8 inhumations had necklaces (graves 1, 2, 4, 17, 21, 41, 51 and 142). They were made up of different numbers of beads (from 13 to 270) and in all more than 800 beads were found in these inhumations.

We can distinguish several types among the glass beads. The majority of the beads were spherical, conical, cylindrical, biconical or annular . The beads were mostly made of dark blue or green glass, there were however also some that were brown, yellow or light blue.

The necklace from grave 4 was made up of 270 small beads of different colours; the one from grave 142 was made of 179 beads and included a cylindrical green glass bead. The necklace from grave 41 was made up of 230 beads of which 215 were small and the rest larger. Among them were conical and spherical ones of green glass (8), biconical beads, polygonal beads of blue glass and divided beads, and four spherical beads containing gold leaf. The other necklaces were made up of a smaller number of beads but their composition was very varied. The necklace from grave 51 was made of 33 beads: most (19) were cylindrical green glass beads, 5 were small green annular beads; there was one conical bead made of blue glass, three spherical beads containing gold leaf, four vase-shaped beads made of bone, and a coiled tube made of bronze wire. There were unusual beads in the necklace from grave 17 (38 beads). The majority were cylindrical and made of black amber engraved with lines (16); besides this there were divided beads made of black paste (5), long biconical beads of blue glass (8), smaller blue conical, biconical and spherical ones (8), green cylindrical or circular beads (1 of each) and lastly two large amber beads, The finest necklace was found in grave 1. It consisted of 33 beads and an ornamental fastening of gold wire. The eleven beads were made from gold-tin alloy, and 2 annular beads were of amber. The rest of the beads were glass, mainly annular and spherical and of light-blue glass (12), with one green one. One large dark blue bead was polygonal, the rest of the larger beads were made from a green or grey-blue glass paste (5). One cylindrical bead was decorated.

In the 15-bead necklace from grave 2, besides the small round beads of dark blue glass (11) there was a larger cylindrical bead made from the same glass, a brown bead of an unusual pear-shape, and 2 bone beads. The necklace from grave 21 contained 13 beads, made up of small round and angular green beads (12), and one large polygonal bead of dark blue glass.

Around the neck of skeleton in grave 70 were the remains of an ornament which can be described as a 'choker'. To the remnants of a leather collar there were fastened small spirals of fine bronze wire, and between them on small wires were hung beads: three were polygonal green glass beads, eight were made from blue glass in the shape of a drop, and the rest were spherical beads of white paste. The ornament was probably in the shape of a fairly narrow leather collar, decorated with small wire spirals and small beads which were sewn on to it, and the whole band was fastened round the neck.

It is clear from this survey that a wide variety of beads was used for necklaces. The most popular were beads made from green or blue glass; the bead of brown glass was unique. Comparatively precious were beads made from transparent glass with a gold-leaf underlay. In addition beads were made from opaque paste in either green, grey-blue or black. Only one bead made of paste was decorated. Only rarely were beads made from other materials. The most expensive were small beads made from thin gold foil. Amber beads had the simple shape of a flattened ball. Cylindrical bone beads were found, together with more complicated vase-like shapes probably manufactured on a lathe. Among the valuable beads were some of black amber, found in only one necklace.

Gold beads from inhumations at Intercisa are depicted by M. Alföldi. This cemetery also produced beads of black amber.[135]

In the Rusovce burials there were found 12 rings of several types. From grave 102 came 2 plain rings made of bronze wire. In graves 41 and 102 (fig. 74, no. 5) there were undecorated rings made from bronze-plate. There were 2 rings in grave 53 made from a bronze band with one end beaten out. In grave 102 there was a ring consisting of a band with a plain flat bezel.

The most interesting group consisted of rings of bronze or silver with a bezel. The bronze ring from grave 12 had a bezel on which was neatly engraved a stylised bird with its head facing back (fig. 74, no. 4). The bronze ring from grave 14 had an opal inset made of two parts on which a bust was engraved (fig. 74, no. 6). A silver ring from grave 41 had an inset made of light blue glass also with an engraving of a bust (fig. 74, no. 7). A silver ring from grave 144 had a stone inset in the bezel. Owing to damage it was not possible to ascertain the type of stone (fig. 74, no. 8).

From grave 142 came a fragmentary ring of white metal which probably had a bezel. A fragment of an iron ring was found in grave 53. These rings were of various diameters, varying from 1.6 to 2.4 cm, depending on whether the ring belonged to a child or to an adult.

Ornamental rings with a bezel or inset obviously reflected the status of their owners. In every case these rings were found with coins, and in the majority of cases in male inhumations. The ring with the opal intaglio in grave 14 was dated to the first half of the 4th century by coins of Constantine I. The silver ring in grave 41 was dated by coins of Constans to the middle of the 4th century. It is remarkable that this, the largest ring (diameter 2.4 cm) was worn by a woman. The silver ring in grave 144 was dated to the second half of the 4th century by coins of Constantius II. The ring with the bird from grave 12 was dated to the second half of the 4th century by coins of Valens.

Among the finds from Intercisa were rings of various types, among them rings with bezels or insets, similar to the rings found at Rusovce. M.

Alföldi considered the rings with round bezels to be late. She dated them together with the sealing rings, which have a bezel with a reversed engraving, to the middle of the 4th century.[136] At Rusovce some of the rings with an engraved bezel dated from the first half of the 4th century.

Special mention should be made of the silver ring from grave 25 (fig. 74, no.9). It had on its outside small rounded plates which were engraved with letters forming the inscription U SILVANVM VIATOREM completed by a swastika. It was 3 cm in diameter, so it was larger than the other rings. It was not found on a finger but lay by the head as if it had been put into the grave as an afterthought. It was found in the grave of a man, together with coins of Licinius: this dates it to the first half of the 4th century.

The inscription on the ring (SILVANVM VIATOREM) can be explained in various ways. The name Silvanus occurs in Pannonia in inscriptions on tomb-stones. The names Silvanus and Viator are however used as cognomina: in inscriptions on the ring we do not actually have the personal name (praenomen), or the family name (nomen gentilis), but two cognomina next to each other, which excludes this type of explanation.[137]

Another possibility is that Silvanus is used as name and Viator as a description of a function, Viator meaning not only 'traveller' but also an official messenger.

However, a third explanation seems the most feasible: namely that the ring with the inscription was a cult object. If that is so, the ring is evidence of the religious life of the inhabitants of the region in the 4th century. Silvanus an ancient Roman god of the forest who was also the guardian of gardens and herds of cattle. The inhabitants of Pannonia worshipped mainly Silvanus, besides paying homage to the official cults of Jupiter, Juno and Minerva. E. Swoboda writes that Silvanus, the chief deity of the original inhabitants of Pannonia, managed to keep his unique position throughout the Roman period.[138]

Objects connected with the cult of Silvanus have been found on numerous sites in Pannonia. These are mostly altars with inscriptions, but there are also small objects such as rings. Altars, sculptures, reliefs and objects consecrated to Silvanus have mostly been found in Roman villas. Among these are inscriptions to "Silvano Silvestri" and "Silvano Domestico".[139] Two altars were found in the neighbourhood of Brigetio with dedications to Silvanus; a third altar was dedicated to Silvanus Domesticus.[140] In Aquincum, 35 stone altars were found associated with the cult of Silvanus, the greatest number dating from the first half of the 3rd century. In recent years two altars were discovered in excavations, one inscribed Silvano Silvestro and the other Silvani Silvestri.[141] A fragment of an altar was found in Intercisa inscribed Silvano Deo Sancto. In Gorsium there was found a relief depicting Silvanus and inscribed Silvanus Domesticus.[142] E. Swoboda mentions 2 altars dedicated to Silvanus found in Carnuntum; one bore the inscription Silvanus Silvester. He mentions that in recent years 4 altars dedicated to Silvanus were found in the town.[143] In the cemetery at Keszthelyi a silver ring was found in an inhumation with the inscription STE SILVANE.[144]

The above examples show that the Roman Silvanus also had the attributes of Silvester and Domesticus. On the ring from Rusovce there was a further title, that of Viator.

The bracelets found in inhumations at Rusovce were made of bronze, iron or bone. The commonest were the bronze bracelets, of which several types could be distinguished. The simplest was the closed bracelet made from a round wire, as that from grave 3 (fig. 85, no. 1). There was a similar bracelet made of a rod of circular cross-section with thickened ends in grave 2 (fig. 85, no. 4). A bracelet made from thin wire was found in grave 41; originally its now open ends were probably furnished with a hook and eye (fig. 85, no. 2). We find that a hook and eye fastening is used on bracelets made of twisted wire, several of which were found (grave 41, 3 examples; grave 52, 1 example; fig. 85, nos. 5, 8). The rest of the bracelets were open and their ends were decorated in various ways. The bracelet from grave 36 was made from a thin rod with the ends flattened out and decorated with stamped circles (fig. 85, no. 3). The rectangular ends of the bracelet from grave 55 had incised decoration (fig. 85, no. 9). The ends of the two bracelets from grave 14 were flattened and had an incised decoration of lines and ring-and-dot, which may be the stylised head of a snake (fig. 85, nos. 6, 7). The ends of the bracelet from grave 41 had quite definite stylised heads of snakes (fig. 85, no. 10). The fragment of a bracelet from grave 1 had the form of a narrow band with a zigzag design; in this case it is impossible to say whether the bracelet was closed or open (fig. 85, no. 11).

The measurements of the bracelets were more or less the same; their diameter was usually 6 cm; two were 6.5 cm in diameter and there were 2 smaller ones with diameters of 5.5 cm.

The iron bracelets were so corroded that only fragments remained (graves 14 and 71). Only in grave 3 was it possible to measure the iron bracelet in situ; it was 6 cm in diameter, and was made of a small iron rod around which was wound bronze wire.

Bracelets made of bone survived only as fragments. In grave 36 there was a closed, undecorated bracelet, its oval ends joined with 2 bronze rivets (fig. 85, no. 12). A similar simple bracelet came from grave 41. In grave 21 were found fragments of a bracelet decorated with an encircling groove (fig. 85, no. 13). A fragment of a more massive bone bracelet from grave 2 was decorated with diagonal grooves (fig. 85, no. 14).

Only an approximate assessment of the size of the fragmentary bracelets can be made; they appear to have been oval, 7 x 6 cm to 7 x 8 cm in diameter.

M. Alföldi has described the bracelets of various materials found at Intercisa. She divided the bronze bracelets into two main types: those made of wire and those made of a metal strip. Among the bracelets made of wire were those made of several twisted wires with hook and eye fastening, like the bracelets from graves 41 and 52 at Rusovce. This type of bracelet began in the 3rd century and was in use in the 4th century. According to the author the most popular type in the second half of the 4th century was that made from a bronze rod with decorated ends, similar to those from graves 14 and 41 at Rusovce. M. Alföldi states that the bracelets with the heads of snakes and those made of a wire wound round a rod were typical grave-goods in Pannonia in the second third of the 4th century.[145]

The bone bracelets found at Intercisa were decorated with engraved lines and rings. M. Alföldi considers these bracelets to be a typical item of womens' dress. Alföldiova considers these bracelets to be a typical item of womens' dress. She dates them to the latter part of the 4th century and seeks their origins in the Western provinces.[146]

It is surprising that no ear-rings were found at Rusovce, although various types were found in inhumations of the 4th century on other sites (e.g. in Ságvár and Intercisa cemeteries). The single small earring found at Rusovce in grave 21 was made of gold wire (plate V, no. 1). This simple type of ear-ring was also found in the cemetery at Intercisa, where a number of gold ear-rings were found. Ear-rings of this type made of gold and bronze wire were also found at Ságvár.[147]

A fragment of bronze plate of unknown use was found in grave 5 decorated with a punched and incised decoration, and was fastened with flat rivets (fig. 85, no. 15). R. Koch has discussed similar late Roman plates and describes close parallels with the Rusovce find. His were bronze plates from Weinheim (Germany) and he considers them to be parts of a set belonging to a belt. In his opinion belt plates with punched decoration date from $\underline{c}$. 400. These belts formed part of the military dress and were popular on the Rhine and Danube frontiers.[148] The plate from grave 5 was of this type and had the same style of decoration as those from Weinheim. The details of the ornament were however different.

Buckles of bronze or iron were part of the male dress. Two bronze buckles were found in graves 30 and 32, and two iron ones in grave 18. These buckles were mostly oval and were joined with a double plate to which the belt was attached (graves 30 and 32). The oval buckles from graves 12 and 30 were preserved without plates. In graves 31 and 140 both bronze buckles were circular and had iron pins. The buckle from grave 31 had two protuberances for the attachment of the belt (Plate IV, nos. 1, 4, 5).

The majority of the oval bronze buckles had iron pins, only the buckles from graves 12 and 32 being made entirely of bronze. The diameter of the bronze buckles was usually 2.4-3.5 cm, the iron ones being generally larger with a diameter of 3.5-5.6 cm. The iron buckles were also either oval (graves 18, 46 and 144) or circular (graves 34 and 102). (Plate IV, nos. 2, 3, 6).

MISCELLANEOUS

Only one bone comb was found in the Rusovce cemetery, in grave 5. This double-sided comb was made from three plates joined by six bronze rivets, the sides of the plates being decorated with engraved concentric circles (fig. 85, no.16). This skilfully made type of comb points to a later Roman date. Combs, made of bone, of Roman date were discussed by S. Thomas who described, however, only the one-sided three-layer type; she did not include in her discussion the double-sided combs.[149] M. Lamiová-Schmiedlová dates the double-sided three-layer comb from Šebastovce to the 4th century.[150] A fragment of a three-layer comb from Kapušany decorated with concentric rings, was dated to the 5th century. V. Budinský-Krička dated a double-sided comb from Levice also to the 5th century.[151]

As no objects from the 5th century were found at Rusovce we have to date the comb from grave 5 to the late 4th century. This dating is supported by finds at Intercisa of three-layer double-sided combs made of bone which, according to M. Alföldi, were in use in this area from the beginning of the 4th century.[152]

Only a few small objects of daily use were found in the inhumations. The vessel made from bronze plate with a shallow lid and a chain, from grave 167, was an ink-pot (atramentarium, Plate VI , no. 2). A bronze ink-pot of the same shape and size was found at Intercisa, but had a tin lid with a chain. A. Radnoti writes that an ink-pot was quite often included among the grave-goods in inhumations.[153] It is quite likely that the lid from grave 12 at Rusovce came from a similar ink-pot: the associated cylindrical vessel, 6 cm high, obviously made from some organic material, had disintegrated. The lid was of the same shape and size (diameter 3.5 cm) as the lids of the other ink-pots. Both these ink-pots lay in male graves in association with brooches. Coins of Valens dated grave 12 to the middle of the 4th century.

An isolated find was a rectangular whetstone from the male inhumation in grave 25. From grave 18 there came a biconical pendant of unknown purpose (Plate VI, no. 3).

In the female burial 1 was found a small annular disc made of tin plate decorated with moulded pattern of a wavy line and rings (fig. 85 , no.17). It was the frame of a mirror which had been lost. A number of mirror frames were discovered at Intercisa: J. Fitz divided them into several types according to shape and decoration. Intercisa Type IX affords the closest parallel to the Rusovce frame, but it differs slightly in its decoration. J. Fitz dates the group of mirror frames with the tendril-like decoration to the 3rd-4th centuries; in his opinion this style of decoration is of Eastern origin. According to him the small size of the mirror (diameter c. 3 cm) made it impractical to use and its function was almost that of an amulet or of a gift to the deceased. He states that the frames were mostly made of tin and in this connection he reminds us of the magical and curative properties of that metal.[154]

Also in women's graves nos. 21 and 41 there were bone spindle-whorls (Plate VI, no. 4). The diameters of these biconical spindle-whorls were 3.3 and 3.5 cm. M. Alföldi[155] recorded a similar spindle-whorl from Intercisa.

IRON OBJECTS

A comparatively small number of iron objects were found in the inhumations at Rusovce; of these only two types were represented, namely knives and awls. In this period iron weapons were no longer used as grave-goods. Iron knives were usually found in male burials. They had a straight blade and a tang which accounted for roughly a third of the whole length. They fell into two groups according to size: the shorter ones were 8-11 cm long and 1.8-3 cm wide (graves 25, 31, 7 and 102), and the bigger ones were 15.5-19 cm long and 2-3.5 cm wide (graves 32, 84, 103 and 140). Traces of wood were generally visible on the tang, derived from the handle; the knife from grave 84 had a wooden sheath.

In some of the graves there was an iron awl as well as a knife (graves 7, 9, 102 and 103). The iron part of the awl which was preserved was on average 9-9.6 cm long. Some traces of the wooden handle usually survived on the tang. The pointed iron object from grave 144 was probably a tool; it was 15 cm long and could have been a punch with an iron handle.

Groups of iron hobnails with hemispherical heads were found in graves where the body was orientated with its head to the south-east. The nails were always found near the lower limbs. In grave 37 there was a dark oval stain by the left knee measuring 30 x 11 cm and roughly 4 cm deep on which lay 55 iron nails. In grave 56 there was a long dark stain beside the femur, 38 x 8 cm in area, on which lay 3 layers of iron nails one above another: 118 nails are preserved; in one layer there were about 40 such nails. In grave 63 there was a dark stain beside the femur, 25 x 7 x 5 cm deep, where there were three layers of iron hobnails numbering 38 in all; 2 more nails were found near the heel. By the left femur were 34 similar nails in three layers but in one row. Altogether 74 nails were found by the legs. In grave 67 there was a row of nails beside the femur and between the femurs were two rows of nails placed diagonally; lower down was yet another row; altogether 64 nails were preserved.

In grave 58 there were ten hobnails by the end of the left leg, in grave 66 eighteen nails were found by the left tibia. Lastly in grave 119, in the corners of the grave by the legs there were dark stains 13-15 cm in diameter; on these lay iron hobnails in 2 rows (11 and 9 nails respectively).

We assume that the dark stains were remains of some organic matter, probably leather footwear the soles of which were studded with iron hobnails. On a brick in grave 36 was preserved the imprint of a military shoe, the sole of which was covered with hobnails with hemispherical heads. They were placed around the circumference of the sole and in two rows up the middle. In this case there were 110 nails on the sole. Further footprints on this and on other bricks were less clear and the numbers of nails could not be established.

Iron hobnails occurred in inhumations in various numbers from 10 to 118, possibly because different numbers of nails were used for the manufacture of different styles of footwear. In some instances where groups of nails were fused together by rust they formed curved lines, indicating that they were from either the toe or the heel of the shoe. Leather boots with iron hobnails was part of the military equipment (caligae), and graves where iron nails were found can be considered as military inhumations.

When discussing iron objects from the camp in Intercisa, A. Salamon described similar iron hobnails with round heads, which she assumed were used on footwear and also for decorating leather handbags and sheaths for knives.[156]

In some graves iron nails of various sizes were found. Nails from graves 58, 139 and 145, as mentioned above, probably came from wooden coffins.' The circumstances of the finds in other inhumations were not so clear-cut as to enable us to determine the function of the nails. In grave 4, 2 large nails were found (13 cm and 10.5 cm long). There was a nail in grave 38, and a small one in grave 63. The quantity of nails in these graves was insufficient to prove the existence of wooden coffins.

THE DATING OF THE INHUMATIONS

The dating of the Rusovce cemetery is based primarily on the Roman coins in the inhumations. The coins that were identified belonged to the Roman emperors from Maximianus Herculius to Valens (286-378). The period of the inhumations, according to coins, therefore covers roughly 100 years, approximately from the end of the 3rd century to the end of the 4th. The dating of the inhumations to the 4th century is supported by the study of the burial rites and of the other finds.

In the 3rd century, the burial rites in Pannonia were already changing from cremation to inhumation. Examples quoted from cemeteries in Hungary show that tombs built in brick and stone were in use in this province in the 4th century. Hungarian scholars place them mostly in the middle of the 4th century. The onion-shaped bronze brooch was the commonest of all the finds. It was a customary part of a Roman soldier's dress and brooches of this form were used exclusively in the 4th century. It could therefore be safely relied upon for the purposes of dating. Other finds from inhumations verified the 4th century date of the cemetery. From parallels with cemeteries in Hungary, the types of glass vessel from inhumations at Rusovce (cylindrical and conical beakers, and the decorated jug) dated to the 4th century. Some of the earlier pottery types continued to be manufactured (e.g. yellow jugs, and the coarse grey vessels) but pots with a coloured metallic glaze were typical products of the 4th century kilns; this was also confirmed by Hungarian scholars (K. Póczy).

At Rusovce there was a group of inhumations in which the skeletons had their heads orientated to the south-east. This group formed, as it were, a group intermediate between the cremations and the inhumations in which the body was orientated with its head to the north-west. In the cemetery to the east of the gymnasium, not one burial was found with the head of the skeleton pointed south-east. Among the south-east orientated skeletons there was also one, grave 35, containing a knee-shaped brooch, which can be dated to the 3rd century. It is possible that this group of burials, which lay on the edge of the 4th century burial ground, was earlier and still belonged to the second half of the 3rd century. It has been concluded therefore that the overall duration of inhumations at the Rusovce cemetery extended from the second half of the 3rd century to the end of the 4th century.

The question of the dating of the Rusovce cemetery can be conclusively settled on the basis of the grave-goods found there. However, the question of the ethnic and social composition of the population buried there remains uncertain until we have sufficient material from other cemeteries in this district at our disposal. The male inhumation with onion-shaped bronze brooches showed that these were soldiers garrisoned in Roman Gerulata. The burials of women and children testify that this locality was also used as a civilian cemetery for the local community. The small number of children's graves is surprising; probably the children's skeletons were buried in shallower graves and so have been destroyed by cultivation.

It has been mentioned that graves 5 and 36, built in brick and containing several skeletons, were probably family tombs. The observation that the persons buried in these tombs were without grave-goods indicates that they may have been Christians. J. Szilagyi believes that there may have been Christians in Aquincum as early as the first half of the 4th century.[157]

CONCLUSIONS

In considering the results of the excavation of this cemetery, it must be borne in mind that Rusovce is the only locality in the former Roman province of Pannonia where the excavation has been conducted by Slovak archaeologists. Hitherto the evidence relating to the period of Roman rule in the Danube region has been obtained from theleft bank of the river, where the Roman garrisons were surrounded by a barbarian population (Devin, Stupava, Pác, Leányvár, Milanovce). In this excavation there were obtained for the first time numerous remains of the provincial Roman culture, as opposed to isolated, imported, objects.

The analysis of the burial rites and of the finds from the cemetery at Rusovce show that the site consisted of two burial places which differed from one another in the manner of burial and in the accompanying grave-goods. Cremations belonged roughly in the 2nd century, but it is quite possible that some of them extended into the beginning of the 3rd century. The dating was based on finds of coins, glass, lamps, and terra sigillata. The inhumations in ordinary graves or in brick-built tombs can be dated from the second half of the 3rd century to the end of the 4th century. The dating of these burials was confirmed by the finds of Roman coins, and such typical objects as brooches, rings, glass and glazed and burnished pottery. The existence of cemeteries also shows that Gerulata was occupied at least from the second to the fourth centuries.

The finds from the cemetery illustrate burial customs connected with the religious conceptions of the population of that time. The finds reflect the material culture of the native people, and the finds from Rusovce afford a reliable basis for the dating of similar objects found in the adjacent non-Roman regions. It is assumed that the objects found at Rusovce were in daily use by the population, so that the date of manufacture coincided with the date of use. When dating objects acquired from outside the Roman territory, we have to allow a certain time between the actual manufacture of the object, its acquisition and its burial.

It can be said in conclusion that the archaeological research at Rusovce, which lasted several years, not only enriched the collections of the Slovak National Museum with new types of artefacts, but also yielded information relating to these finds and contributed to the understanding of the life of the population from the 2nd to the 4th century.

NOTES

1. Ondrouch, V.: K polohe a dejinám rimanskej Gerulaty. In: SMSS, 43-45, 1949-1951, p. 93.

2. Dějiny lidstva. Římské Impérium, zv. 2, Praha 1936, p. 624, příloha.

3. Pelikán, O.: Slovensko a rímske Impérium, Bratislava 1960, pp. 110, 118. Dekan, J.: Výsledky výskumov v Rusovciach-Gerulate. Referát - Liblice 1971.

4. Ondrouch, V.: op.cit.p. 95.

5. Ibid. p. 97.

6. Kraskovská, L.: Nález rímskeho hrobu v Rusovciach. In: AR, 3, 1951, p. 160, 161, 170.

7. Bónis, E.: Römerzeitliche Gräber in Halimba. In: FA, 12, 1960, pp. 97-99.

8. Fülep, F.: Das Frühkaiserzeitliche Gräberfeld von Vasas. In: AAH, 9, 1958, p. 389.

9. Sági, K.: Die Ausgrabungen im römischen Gräberfeld von Intercisa im Jahre 1949. In: Intercisa I, pp. 63, 64. Sági draws our attention to the fact that according to Roman law the ustrinum should have been situated 500 paces outside the settlement.

10. Sági, K.: op.cit., pp. 65,66.

11. Barkóczi, L.: Die datierten Glasfunde aus dem II. Jahrhundert von Brigetio. In: FA, 18, 1966-1967, fig. 30: 2. Radnóti, A.: Glasgefässe und Glasgegenstände. In: Intercisa II, pl. XXIX: 4. Szilágyi, J.: Aquincum, Budapest 1956, pl. XXV.

12. Radnóti, A.: op.cit. p. 154. Barkóczi, L.: op.cit. p. 78.

13. Barkóczi, L.: op.cit. pp. 74-78, fig. 28: 1; 29: 2, 3.

14. Radnóti, A.: op.cit. pp. 142, 143; pl. XXVI: 2, 3, 6, 9; XXVII: 1; XXVIII: 2, 3.

15. Doppelfeld, O.: Römisches und frankisches Glas in Köln. Köln 1966, fig. 59.

16. Barkóczi, L.: op.cit. fig. 27: 2.

17. Doppelfeld, O.: op.cit. fig. 66.

18. Radnóti, A.: op.cit. pl. XXIX: 9.

19. Ibid. pp. 141, 145.

20. Barkóczi, L.: op.cit. pp. 67, 82.

21. Loeschcke, S.: Lampen aus Vindonissa. Zürich 1919.

22. Iványi, D.: Die pannonischen Lampen. DP, S 2, č. 2. Budapest 1935.

23. Póczy, K.: Lampen. In: Intercisa II, p. 87.

24. Szentléleky, T.: Ancient lamps. Budapest 1969.

25. Neumann, A.: Der römische Limes in Österreich, Lampen und andere Beleuchtungsgeräte aus Vindobona. Wien 1967, pp. 9,10.

26. Loeschcke, S.: op.cit. p. 211.

27. Szentléleky, T.: op.cit. pp. 68, 69, 71, fig. 80.

28. Iványi, D.: op.cit. pp. 10, 11, Pl. XI: 1, 4, 5, 6.

29. Loeschcke, S.: op.cit. p. 243.

30. Szentléleky, T.: op.cit. p. 92.

31. Iványi, D.: op.cit. p. 10. Szentléleky, T.: op.cit. p. 92.

32. Loeschcke, S.: op.cit. p. 255; Pl. XVIII , XIX.

33. Iványi, D.: op.cit. p. 16.

34. Ibid. p. 16. Neumann, A.: op.cit. p. 10.

35. Loeschcke, S.: op.cit. p. 280. Iványi, D.: op.cit. p. 30.
    Szentlékeky, T.: op.cit. p. 92. Póczy, K.: op.cit. pp. 88,128.

36. Szentléleky, T.: op.cit. p. 92.

37. Ibid. p. 92. Loeschcke, S.: op.cit. pp. 262, 282. Iványi, D.: op. cit. p. 16.

38. Iványi, D.: op.cit. pp. 19, 29.

39. Ibid. Pl. L-LII; Pl. LI; 9,11.

40. Neumann, A.: op.cit. fig. 70.

41. Iványi, D.: op.cit. 30, 31; Pl. LXXIX: 1-4; LXXXIII: 3-5;
    LXXXVI: 43-45, 49-67; XCIII: 30-55; XCIV: 74-80; XCVIII: 1-3;
    XCV: 31-34.

42. Iványi, D.: Ibid. pp. 19, 29.

43. Póczy, K.: op.cit. c. 11, Pl. XXIII: 14.

44. Iványi, D.: op.cit. p. 25, Pl. LXV: 8, 14.

45. Póczy, K.: op.cit. p. 90.

46. Dragendorff, H.: Terra Sigillata. In: BJ, 96, 1895.

47. Ludowici, W.: Stempel-Bilder Römischer Töpfer (aus meinen Ausgrabungen in Rheinzabern), 1901-1905, pp. 76, 285.

48. Oswald, F. - Pryce, D.: Terra sigillata. London 1966, pp. 194, 202, 214.

49. Ludowici, W.: op.cit. p. 76.

50. Karnitsch, P.: Die Reliefsigillata von Ovilava. Linz 1959, pp. 31, 32, 76.

51. Ludowici, W.: op.cit. pp. 60, 281.

52. Oswald, F. - Pryce, D.: op.cit. pp. 121, 206.

53. MacDonald, G.: Forschungen in römischen Britannien. In: Neunzehnter BerRGK, Frankfurt am Main 1930, p. 71. Ludowici, W.: op.cit. p. 72 č. 4428; p. 6, č, 4610.

54. Juhász, G.: Die Sigillaten von Brigetio, DP, S 2, č. 3, Pl. IX: 1; XI: 7; X: 13, 14.

55. Póczy, K.: Die Töpferwerkstätten von Aquincum. In: AAH, 7, 1956, p. 126.

56. Juhász, G.: op.cit. Pl. XIV: 14.

57. Bónis, E.: Die Kaiserzeitliche Keramik von Pannonien. I. Die Materialen der frühen Kaiserzeit. DP, S 2, č. 20, Budapest 1942. J. Szilágyi depicts a pottery colander with a handle from Aquincum, made however of grey clay. Szilagyi, J.: op. cit. Pl. X.

58. Bónis, E.: op.cit.

59. Ibid. pp. 41, 119; Pl. XVIII: 25, 27.

60. Ibid. pp. 42, 107, 109; Pl. XVII: 16, 17, 19.

61. Ibid. p. 227; Pl. XXIX: 17.

62. Ibid. pp. 199, 209, 222; Pl. XXVI: 3, 13; XXIX: 1.

63. Schörgendorfer, A.: Die römerzeitliche Keramik der Ostalpenländer. Brünn, München, Wien 1942, p. 53, č. 464.

64. Bónis, E.: op.cit. p. 51; Pl. XXIII. Schörgendorfer, A.: op.cit. pp. 17, 94, 185; Pl. 11: 161, 162.

65. Schörgendorfer, A.: op.cit. p. 111.

66. Bónis, E.: op.cit. p. 48.

67. Schörgendorfer, A.: op.cit. p. 20, č. 194.

68. Bónis, E.: op.cit. pp. 43, 108; Pl. XVII: 18. Schörgendorfer, A.: op.cit. p. 111.

69. Schörgendorfer, A.: op.cit. p. 23, č. 214. Mócsy, A.: Frührömische Gräber in Savaria (Szombathely). In: AÉ, 81, 1954, p. 190; fig. 13: 57, 1.

70. Póczy, K.: Die Töpferwerkstätten von Aquincum. In: AAH, 7, 1956, pp. 73, 74, 135; fig. 4: 3, 5; Pl. IV: 11; Pl. V: 14, 16.

71.	Lamiová-Schmiedlová, M.: Spony z doby rímskej na Slovensku. In: ŠZ AÚSAV, 5, 1961, p. 19.

72.	Radnóti, A.: Möbel und Kastchenbeschläge, Schlosser und Schlüssel. In: Intercisa II, pp. 241-249.

73.	Ibid., pp. 242, 245.

74.	Salamon, A.: Gebrauchsgegenstände und Werkzeuge aus Eisen. In: Intercisa II, pp. 369, 370; Pl. LXX: 1-12; Pl. LXXI: 13,14.

75.	Kraskovská, Ľ.: Výskum rímskej stanice v Rusovciach v rokoch 1961 a 1964. In: ZbSNM-História, 7, 1967, pp. 47, 48, 52; fig. 7: 1-6.

76.	A grey jug was probably buried with the later inhumation.

77.	Radnóti, A.: Glasgefässe und Glasgegenstände, op.cit. p. 154.

78.	Parragi, G.: Neuere spätrömische Funde auf der Bécsi Strasse. In: BR, 21, 1964, p. 238; fig. 39, 40.

79.	Parragi, G.: Weitere Gräber aus der Freilegung in der Glasfabric von Óbuda. In: AÉ, 92, 1965, pp. 46-48.

80.	Parragi, G.: Spätrömische Friedhof in der Bogdáni Strasse. In: BR, 20, 1963, p. 326; fig. 7, 14-16.

81.	Mészáros, Gy.: Ein spätrömisches Ziegelgrab in Szekszárd-Szőlőhegy. In: AÉ, 89, 1962, pp. 84-88; fig. 3, 4.

82.	Lányi, V.: Freilegung des Begräbnisfeldes von Margittelep. In: AReg. 4-5, 1963-1964, p. 220. Fitz, J. - Bánki, Sz. - Lányi, V.: Dritter Bericht über die Ausgrabungen in der römischen Siedlung bei Tac 1961-1962. In: AReg, 4-5, 1963-1964, Pl. LI: 1-8.

83.	Fitz, J.: Floriana. In: Areg, 2-3, 1963, pp. 157, 158; Pl. XLVIII: 1-4.

84.	Vágó, B. E.: Spätrömische Gräber in Intercisa und in Bölcske. In: AÉ, 88, 1961, fig. 5.

85.	Radnóti, A.: op.cit. p. 144; Pl. XXVI: 3.

86.	Ibid., pp. 152-153; Pl. XXXIII: 10. 12.

87.	Burger, A.: The late Roman cemetery at Ságvár. In: AAH, 18, 1966, Pl. 99: 2; Pl. 125: 5, 7, 8.

88.	Ibid. Pl. 115: 2; Pl. 120: 2.

89.	Barkóczi, L. - Salamon, A.: Glasfunde von Ende des 4 und Anfang des 5. Jhr. in Ungarn. In: AÉ, 95, 1968, p. 38.

90.	Doppelfeld, O.: op.cit. p. 50; fig. 82.

91.	Radnóti, A.: op.cit. p. 149; Pl. XXXI: 5.

92.	Burger, A.: op.cit. Pl. 96: 3; Pl. 125: 23.

93.	Doppelfeld, O.: op.cit. fig. 79, 105, 106.

94. Ibid. p. 47.

95. Uzsoki, A.: A Győri Xantus János Muzeum, Führer zur Ausstellung, Győr 1967, p. 34; fig. 7.

96. Thomas, E.: Roman glazed ware ornamental vessels in the Győr Muzeum. In: Arrabona, 3, Győr 1961, pp. 17-32; fig. 8.

97. Fülep, F.: Das Frühkaiserzeitliche Gräberfeld von Vasas, op.cit. pp. 376,377; fig. 3: 3; Pl. IV: 4; fig. 6: 6.

98. Póczy, K.: Keramik. In: Intercisa II, pp. 49, 50.

99. Thomas, E.: Römische Villen in Pannonien. Budapest 1964, Pl. CCIV. Szilágyi, J.: op.cit. Pl. VIII.

100. Schörgendorfer, A.: op.cit. 66, 67, 81, 82; Pl. 46, č. 566, 567; Pl. 47, č. 561.

101. Květ, J.: Myšlenka naturalistických nádob od pravěku do renesance. In: SbNM, I, Praha 1938, pp. 123, 124.

102. Ibid. p. 131.

103. Póczy, K.: op.cit. pp. 80, 82, 83; fig. 40, T 38b.

104. Ibid. p. 83; fig. 42, T 63, 64.

105. Ibid. p. 83; fig. 44, T 87-89; Pl. XV: 15-18.

106. Schörgendorfer, A.: op.cit. p. 58; Pl. 41, č. 506.

107. Bónis, E.: op.cit. p. 223; Pl. XXIX: 8.

108. Póczy, K.: op.cit. Pl. XVII: 4, 14.

109. Ibid. pp. 84, 85; fig. 45, T 93, 94, 94a; Pl. XX: 14-15; Pl. IX:13.

110. Burger, A.: op.cit. Pl. 126: 22, 25. Schörgendorfer, A.: op.cit. p. 26; Pl. 17, č. 243; Pl. 18, č. 245.

111. Póczy, K.: op.cit. p. 44, 45. Burger, A.: op. cit. p. 142.

112. Póczy, K.: op.cit. p. 45; fig. 38, T 9.

113. Ibid. p. 126; fig. 43, T 73a. Schörgendorfer, A.: op.cit p. 63, č. 541.

114. Ibid. p. 22, č. 209.

115. Póczy, K.: op.cit. pp. 72, 76; fig. 48, T 112. Burger, A.: op.cit. p. 141; Pl. 126: 30; fig. 84.

116. Póczy, K.: op.cit. p. 81; fig. 38, T 6. Bónis, E.: op.cit.p. 169; Pl. XXI: 47.

117. Póczy, K.: op.cit. p. 110; Pl. XIX: 13; č. kat. 19.

118. Ibid. p. 72; fig. 39, T 19. Parragi, Gy.: Spätrömische Friedhof in der Bogdáni Strasse, op.cit. fig. 1.

119. Póczy, K.: op.cit. p. 71; fig. 38, T 16; Pl. XVIII: 4.

120. Schörgendorfer, A.: op.cit. p. 5, č. 51; Pl. 4.

121. Burger, A.: op.cit. p. 133; Pl. CVII: 4. Schörgendorfer, A.: op.cit. p. 62, č. 538; Pl. 43.

122. Burger, A.: op.cit. p. 122; Pl. CVII: 5-7.

123. Póczy, K.: op.cit. p. 77. Burger, A.: op.cit. p. 140.

124. Thomas, E.: Römische Villen in Pannonien, op.cit. pp. 321, 322, Pl. CCV.

125. Póczy, K.: op.cit. p. 76.

126. Ibid. pp. 30, 31.

127. Sakář, V.: Spony s cibulovitými knoflíky ve střední Evropě. In: PA, 52, 1961. pp. 432, 435.

128. Svoboda, B.: Čechy a římské Imperium. Praha 1948, p. 167.

129. Sági, K.: op.cit. pp. 92. 95.

130. Sági, K.: Die spätrömische Bevölkerung der Umgebung von Keszthely. In: AAH, 12, 1960, pp. 206, 239.

131. Fitz, J.: Spätrömische Gräber in Ercsi, In: AReg, 2-3, 1963, pp. 159-161.

132. Burger, A.: op.cit. p. 142; Pl. LXXXIX.

133. Beljajev, N. M.: Očerki po vizantijskoj archeologii. I-Fibuly v Vizantii. In: Seminarium Kondakovianum, 3, Praha 1929, pp. 86-89; Pl. XV: 1, 3, 5, 13.

134. Lamiová-Schmiedlová, M.: op.cit. p. 19, Pl. V: 9, 10.

135. Alföldi, M.: Schmucksachen. In: Intercisa II, pp. 441, 452; Pl. LXXXI: 5, 6; fig. 94: 17.

136. Ibid. p. 413; Pl. LXXVII: 2; Pl. LXXVIII: 8.

137. Irmscher, J.: Lexikon der Antike. Leipzig 1971, p. 371. Mócsy, A.: Die Bevölkerung von Pannonien bis zu den Markomannenkriegen. Budapest 1959, pp. 125, 190, 196.

138. Swoboda, E.: Carnuntum. Graz-Köln 1958, p. 162.

139. Thomas, E.: op.cit. pp. 144, 145, 198, 399.

140. Ondrouch, V.: Limes romanus na Slovensku. Bratislava 1938, pp. 39, 40, 46.

141. Szilágyi, J.: op.cit. p. 108. Wellner, J.: Ein weiteres Denkmal des Mithras-Kultes aus Aquincum. In: BR, 21, 1964, p. 260; fig. 12. Ürögdi, G.: Spuren von Bankgeschäften in Aquincum. In: BR, 21, 1964, p. 244; fig. 1.

142. Erdélyi, G. - Fülep, F.: Katalog der Steindenkmäler. In: Intercisa I, p. 326, č. 356.

143. Swoboda, E.: op.cit. pp. 142, 150, 245.

144. Sági, K.: Die spätrömische Bevölkerung der Umgebung von Keszthely,
op.cit. p. 244.

145. Alföldi, M.: op.cit. pp. 418, 419, 421; fig. 88, 89.

146. Ibid. pp. 484, 485; Pl. LXXXIV: 15-17.

147. Sági, K.: Die Ausgrabungen in römischen Gräberfeld von Intercisa,
op.cit. p. 79; Pl. XXI: 19, 20. Burger, A.: op.cit. pp. 102, 130;
Pl. 95, grave 24: 4; Pl. 117, grave 294: 3.

148. Koch, R.: Die spätkaiserzeitliche Gürtelgarnitur von der Ehrenburg
bei Forchheim (Oberfranken). In: Germania, 43, 1965, pp. 108, 115,
117; Pl. 13: 4.

149. Thomas, S.: Studien zu den germanischen Kämmen des römischen
Kaiserzeit. In: Arbeits- und Forschungsberichte zur sächsichen
Bodendenkmalpflege, 8, Leipzig 1960, pp. 56-64.

150. Lamiová-Schmiedlová, M.: Hrebene z doby rímskej a stahovania
národov z východného Slovenska. In: Archeologické studijní
materiály ČsAV, 1, Praha 1964, p. 199; fig. 3: 4.

151. Budinský-Krička, V.: Hroby z doby rímskej a stahovania národov v
Kapušanoch. In: SIA, 5, 1957, pp. 356, 359; fig. 1: 2. Budinský-
Krička, V.: Prehistorické a ranodejinné nálezy v Leviciach. In:
AR, 2, 1950, pp. 153, 154; fig. 98.

152. Alföldi, M.: Knochengegenstände. In: Intercisa II, p. 479; fig. 109.

153. Radnóti, A.: Gefässe, Lampen und Tintenfässer aus Bronze. In:
Intercisa II, p. 209; Pl. XLI: 4.

154. Fitz, J.: Bleigegenstände. In: Intercisa II, pp. 384-392; Pl.
LXXIV: 4.

155. Alföldi, M.: op.cit. p. 483.

156. Salamon, A.: Gebrauchgegenstände und Werkzeuge aus Eisen. In:
Intercisa II, p. 373; Pl. LXX: 26, 27.

157. Szilágyi, J.: op.cit. p. 113.

CATALOGUE OF GRAVES

Grave 1, skeleton grave of a woman.

Finds: glass goblet, fig. 73:3; small glass jug, fig. 74:3, necklace of golden beads (11) and glass beads (22) pl. VI:1; bronze bracelet, fig. 85:11; small frame of a mirror, fig. 85:17; bowl, as fig. 78:15; small jug, fig. 78:8; small amphora, fig. 81:9; small vase, fig. 80:9.

Grave 2, skeleton grave of a woman, tomb built of bricks.

Finds: small glass flask, fig. 72:11; small glass flask, fig. 73:1; necklace of glass beads (13) and bone beads (2); bronze bracelet, fig. 85:4; bone bracelet, fig. 85:14; coins: Constantine I (3), Constantine II (2), Constans (1); bowl, as fig. 78:15; jug, fig. 80:3.

Grave 3, skeleton grave.

Finds: glass goblet, fig. 73:4; small glass bottle, fig. 72:9; bronze bracelet, fig. 85:1; fragment of an iron bracelet; iron knife; coin: Constantine I (1); bowl, as fig. 78:15; folded beaker, fig. 79:1.

Grave 4, skeleton grave of a woman.

Finds: glass bottle, fig. 73:4; necklace of glass beads, (270); small jug, fig. 78:9; pot, fig. 81:13; iron nails (2).

Grave 5, skeleton grave (3 skeletons: 1 man, 1 woman and 1 unidentified), tomb built of stone.

Finds: bone comb, fig. 85:16; bronze fitting, fig. 85:15.

Grave 6, skeleton grave, damaged.

Finds: jug, fig. 79:2; brick with stamp LEG XIIII.

Grave 7, skeleton grave of a man.

Finds: bronze fibula, fig. 83:2; broken glass goblet; iron knife and awl; fragment of a 4th century coin; small jug, as fig. 78:8; bowl, as 78:15; fragment of terra sigillata, fig. 76:2.

Grave 8, damaged.

Finds: small jug, fig. 78:7; vessel, bowl.

Grave 9, skeleton grave of a man.

Finds: glass goblet, fig. 73:8; bronze fibula, fig. 82:1; coins: Galerius Maximianus (2); iron point; folded beaker, as fig. 79:1; bowl, as fig. 78:15.

Grave 10, skeleton grave of a man.

Finds: bronze fibula, fig. 82:2; coin: Maximianus Herculius; small jug, as fig. 78:9; bowl, as fig. 78:15.

Grave 11, skeleton grave of a child, tomb built in brick.

Finds: coin: Valens; vessel, fig. 79:3; cup, fig. 81:10.

Grave 12, skeleton grave of a man.

Finds: bronze fibula, fig. 83:3; bronze ring, fig. 74:4; bronze buckle, coins: Valens (2); glass cup, as fig. 73:5; bronze cover.

Grave 13, skeleton grave, tomb built, damaged, without finds.

Grave 14, skeleton grave.

Finds: bronze bracelet, fig. 85:6,7; bronze ring, fig. 74:6; fragment of an iron bracelet; coins: Constantine I (4), Delmatius (1); jug, damaged; bowl, 79:8.

Grave 15, skeleton grave of a man.

Finds: fibula of bronze, fig. 83:4; jug with lip, fig. 80:6; glass cup, fig. 73:5.

Grave 16, skeleton grave, without finds.

Grave 17, skeleton grave.

Finds: necklace of glass beads (36) and beads of yellow amber (2); coins: Constantine I (2), Licinius I (2); jug, fig. 79:7; bowl, as fig. 79:10.

Grave 18, skeleton grave of a man?

Finds: bronze pendant, pl. VI:3; iron clasps (2), pl. VI:6; coins, destroyed (2); anthropomorphic vessel, fig. 81:4; small jug, fig. 78:18; bowl, fig. 78:16.

Grave 19, skeleton grave.

Finds: jug, fig. 80:5; small pot, as fig. 78:12; bowl, fig. 80:2.

Grave 20, skeleton grave of a man, tomb built.

Finds: bronze fibula, fig. 84:1.

Grave 21, skeleton grave of a woman (2 bricks).

Finds: small ear-ring of gold, pl. V:1; necklace of glass beads (13); bone bracelet, fig. 85:13; bone spindle whorl, pl. VI:4; glass goblet (broken), small jug, as fig. 78:7; bowl, fig. 78:16.

Grave 22, skeleton grave of a man, without finds.

Grave 23, skeleton grave, without finds.

Grave 24, damaged, (bricks).

Grave 25, skeleton grave of a man.

Finds: bronze fibula, fig. 82:5; silver ring, fig. 74:9; coins: Licinius I (4); small iron knife, pl. IV:11; whetstone; small jug, fig. 78:9; bowl, fig. 78:17.

Grave 26, skeleton grave without finds.

Grave 27, cremation grave.

Finds: pot, as fig. 81:13; jug, as fig, 78:1; small jug, as fig. 78:7; small jug, as fig. 80:10; bowl, as fig, 78:16; spindle whorl; iron nails (2).

Grave 28, skeleton grave.

Finds: coin, damaged; jug, fig. 80:4; iron hooked nails (2).

Grave 29, skeleton grave.

Finds: bronze fibula, fig. 82:4; coin: Constantius Chlorus; iron hooked nail; vase, fig. 81:5; goblet, fig. 81:3; bowl, fig. 78:15.

Grave 30, skeleton grave of a man.

Finds: glass goblet, broken; bronze buckle, pl. IV:1; bronze buckle; coins: Constantine I (1), Constantius II (2); Helena; iron knife; bowl, fig. 80:1.

Grave 31, skeleton grave of a child.

Finds: bronze buckle, pl. IV:5; coins: Licinius I, Constantine II; small iron knife, pl. IV:10; small jug, fig. 80:10; bowl, as fig. 78:17.

Grave 32, skeleton grave of a man.

Finds: bronze fibula, fig. 82:3; bronze buckle, pl. IV:4; bronze buckle, coins: Valerius Severus, Valeria, Constantine I (2), Licinius I; iron knife, pl. IV:13; glass goblet (broken); jug with lip, as fig. 79:5; bowl, as fig. 78:16.

Grave 33, skeleton grave, without finds.

Grave 34, skeleton grave.

Finds: iron buckle; amphora, fig. 80:8.

Grave 35, skeleton grave.

Finds: bronze fibula, fig. 82:6.

Grave 36, skeleton grave with 2 skeletons of women, tomb built: 2 bricks with stamps of LEG XIIII G and tegula, pl. VI:11.

Finds: small glass vase, fig. 74:2; bronze bracelet, fig. 85:3; bone bracelet, fig. 85:12; small goblet, fig. 81:8; small jug, as fig. 78:7.

Grave 37, skeleton grave.

Finds: jug, as fig. 80:5; small iron knife; iron nail from boot.

Grave 38, skeleton grave.

Finds: iron nail.

Grave 39, skeleton grave, tomb built.

Finds: iron fragment.

Grave 40, skeleton grave.

Finds: iron knife, pl. IV:12.

Grave 41, skeleton grave of a woman.

Finds: necklace of glass beads (230); bronze bracelet, fig. 85:10; bronze bracelet, fig. 85:2; bronze bracelets (3), fig. 85:5; bone bracelet, broken; silver ring, fig. 74:7; bronze ring, fig. 74:5; coins:

Constans, (2); bone spindle whorl, damaged; jug with lip, as fig. 79:4; bowl, as fig. 78:16.

Grave 42, skeleton grave.

Finds: jug with lip, as fig. 79:5; bowl, as fig. 78:16.

Grave 43, skeleton grave, tomb built in brick, brick with stamp of LEG XIIII G.

Finds: fragment of glass.

Grave 44, skeleton grave without finds.

Grave 45, skeleton grave without finds.

Grave 46, skeleton grave.

Finds: iron clasp, pl. IV:3; small iron knife.

Grave 47, skeleton grave of a man.

Finds: glass fragment; jug, as fig, 80:5; small jug with lip, fig. 80:7; small pot, fig. 78:12.

Grave 48, skeleton grave.

Finds: iron awl, pl. IV:17; fragment of a bronze needle; pot, as fig. 78:12; potsherd.

Grave 49, skeleton grave, damaged.

Grave 50, damaged.

Grave 51, skeleton grave of a woman.

Finds: necklace of glass beads (28) and bone beads (4), glass cup (broken); iron nails.

Grave 52, skeleton grave of a man.

Finds: glass bottle (broken); bronze bracelet, fig. 85:8; jug with lip, as fig. 79:5; bowl, as fig. 78:16.

Grave 53, skeleton grave of a woman.

Finds: glass goblet, fig. 74:1; small glass flask, fig. 72:10; bronze rings (2) pl. V:4; fragment of an iron ring; jug, fig. 79:6; bowl, as fig. 78:15.

Grave 54, cremation grave.

Finds: oil lamp, as pl. V:11; small pot, fig. 77:5, potsherd of jug; iron nails (2).

Grave 55, skeleton grave of a man (bricks).

Finds: bronze bracelet, fig. 85:9; small vase, fig. 81:6; jug, fig. 81:1.

Grave 56, skeleton grave of a man.

Finds: jug, as fig. 80:5; bowl, fig. 78:14, iron nails from boots.

Grave 57, skeleton grave, without finds.

Grave 58, skeleton grave of a man.

Finds: iron nails (4), iron nails from boots.

Grave 59, cremation grave.

Finds: jug, as fig. 78:1; pot, as fig. 77:5.

Grave 60, cremation grave.

Finds: oil lamp, as pl. V:11, and fig. 75:14; potsherd, iron nail.

Grave 61, skeleton grave without discoveries.

Grave 62, skeleton grave, without finds, damaged.

Grave 63, skeleton grave of a man.

Finds: jug, as fig. 79:6; bowl, fig. 78:17, iron nail, iron nails from boots.

Grave 64, cremation grave.

Finds: potsherd.

Grave 65, cremation grave.

Finds: folded beaker, fig. 77:8; small vase, fig. 78:6; terra sigillata bowl,
    fig. 77:2; small glass jug, fig. 72:6.

Grave 66, skeleton grave.

Finds: iron nails from boots. The rubbish was from the cremation grave 66a:
    oil lamp, pl. V:9, 10, fig. 75:13; jug fragment.

Grave 67, skeleton grave.

Finds: iron nails from boots, fragment of a nail.

Grave 68, cremation grave.

Finds: oil lamp, as pl. V:11; small glass flask, fig. 72:8; bronze fittings
    (2), iron nail; iron fragments (2), iron nails from boots; bowl;
    fragment of a vessel; jug fragment.

Grave 69, cremation grave.

Finds: coins: Faustina I; damaged coin; bronze fitting , fig. 85:19;
    iron nail from boots; fragment of an oil lamp, fig. 75:17.

Grave 70, skeleton grave of a woman.

Finds: necklace with beads; coin: Constantine II; fragment of an iron brace-
    let; goblet; fig. 81:2; jug with lip, fig. 79:5; bowl, as fig. 78:15.

Grave 71, skeleton grave.

Finds: vessel, fig. 80:11; fragment of an iron bracelet; fragment of a
    vessel.

Grave 72, cremation grave.

Finds: glass bottle, fig. 72:1; coin: Hadrian; oil lamp, as pl. V:9; iron
    nail, fragment of a jug; fragment of a pot.

Grave 73, cremation grave.

Finds: small zoomorphic vessel of glass, fig. 72:2; iron fittings from a chest, pl. IV:18.

Grave 74, cremation grave.

Finds: coin: Hadrian; oil lamp, as pl. V:11, and fig. 75:15; iron nails from boots; jug, fig. 78:1; potsherds.

Grave 75, cremation grave.

Finds: oil lamp, as pl. V:11, fig. 75:10; iron nail: fragment of a vessel; sherd of a bowl.

Grave 76, cremation grave.

Finds: iron fragment (2); iron nail; fragment of a jug.

Grave 77, cremation grave.

Finds: iron nails (2); fragment of a jug.

Grave 78: cremation grave.

Finds: bowl, as an imitation of the terra sigillata, fig. 77:3; fragment of a vessel; fragments of a jug (2), sherd of a folded beaker; sherd of a small bowl; sherd of a strainer, pl. VI:10.

Grave 79, no remains.

Finds: iron fragments.

Grave 80, cremation grave.

Finds: oil lamp, as pl. V:9; iron nails, iron nails from boots; sherds of a jug.

Grave 81, cremation grave.

Finds: coin: Hadrian; iron nails; iron nails from boots; oil lamp, as pl. V:16, fig. 75:3; jug, as fig. 78:1.

Grave 82, skeleton grave.

Finds: jug with lip, as fig. 79:5; sherd of a vessel, painted over; fragment of a pot.

Grave 83, skeleton grave, without finds.

Grave 84, skeleton grave of a man.

Finds: bronze fibula, fig. 83:1; coin: Licinius I; iron knife; small jug, as fig. 78:10.

Grave 85, skeleton grave of a child, without finds.

Grave 86, cremation grave.

Finds: iron nail; fragment of a jug, as fig. 78:1.

Grave 87, cremation grave.

Finds: damaged coin; iron nails (2); oil lamp, as pl. V:11; fig. 75:1; bowl of terra sigillata, fig. 77:1.

Grave 88, cremation grave.

Finds: fragment of a vessel; iron nails.

Grave 89, cremation grave.

Finds: sherds of a vessel; iron nail.

Grave 90, no remains?

Finds: bowl, as an imitation of the terra sigillata, fig. 77:4; fragment of a
vessel; fragments of terra sigillata.

Grave 91, cremation grave.

Grave 92, cremation grave.

Finds: fragments of an ornament of bronze, pl. IV:7; iron fragment, iron
nail, glass bottle, fig. 72:4;   fused glass beads? fragment of
an oil lamp, pot, fig. 78:3; sherd of a jug, sherd of a small bowl,
sherd of a vessel.

Grave 93, cremation grave.

Finds: fragment of a jug.

Grave 94, cremation grave, probably a place for the cremation of the dead
bodies.

Finds: various iron nails (9), iron nails from boots, fragments of bronze,
and a nail, fragment of glass, smelted glass, oil lamp, as pl. V:11,
fig. 75:18; bowl of terra sigillata, as fig. 77:1, sherd of a vessel
and a bowl.

Grave 95, cremation grave.

Finds: iron fittings from a chest, pl. IV:19; iron nails (2), iron nails from boots,
fragment of a jug, sherds of a vessel, fragment of a pot.

Grave 96, cremation grave.

Finds: fragment of a bronze fibula, fig. 85:18, fittings of bronze, pl. IV:8,
iron nails from boots, oil lamp, as pl. V:11, fragment of an oil lamp,
fragment of a jug, as fig. 78:1; sherd of a vessel, sherd of a bowl.

Grave 97, cremation grave.

Finds: damaged coin, iron nail, oil lamp, pl. V:11, 12, fig. 75:20, sherd of
a jug, sherd of a small pot, sherd of a vessel, melted glass beads.

Grave 98, cremation grave.

Finds: coin: Antoninus Pius, oil lamp, as pl. V:16, sherd of a small pot.

Grave 99, cremation grave.

Finds: glass bottle, fig. 72:5, oil lamp, as pl. V:11, fig. 75:22, jug with lip,
fig. 77:10, small pot, fig. 77:7, iron fragment.

Grave 100, cremation grave.

Finds: sherds of 3 vessels.

Grave 101, cremation grave, the roof of bricks.

Finds: iron nails (2), sherd of a jug, sherd of a bowl.

Grave 102, skeleton grave of a child.

Finds: glass goblet, fig. 73:6, bronze rings (4), iron buckle, iron knife, as pl. IV:9, iron awl, as pl. IV:16; small vase, fig. 81:7, jug, fig. 79:9.

Grave 103, skeleton grave of a man.

Finds: glass goblet, as fig. 73:7, bronze fibula, fig. 84:2, bronze ring, small ring of bronze, iron knife, pl. IV:9, iron awl, pl. IV:16. There was in the infilling cremation grave 103, with associated finds: oil lamp, fig. 75:12, sherds of a vessel.

Grave 104, cremation grave.

Finds: oil lamp, pl. V:6, fragment of a jug.

Grave 105, cremation grave.

Finds: small vessel of glass, fig. 72:7, coin: Hadrian, iron lock? pl. IV:14; iron nail, oil lamp, as pl. V:11, small flagstone, sherd of a jug.

Grave 106, cremation grave.

Finds: iron nails (2), sherds.

Grave 107, cremation grave.

Finds: fragment of a jug, sherd of a strainer,

Grave 108, cremation grave.

Finds: oil lamp, pl. V:7,8, fig. 75:24, small iron knife, iron nails (5).

Grave 109, cremation grave.

Finds: small jug, fig. 78:4.

Grave 110, cremation grave.

Finds: oil lamp, pl. V:13, fig. 75:5, jug, fig. 78:2, fragment of a vessel.

Grave 111, cremation grave?

Finds: fragment of a vessel (2).

Grave 112, cremation grave.

Finds: fragments of an iron ring, iron knife, iron nail, iron nails from boots, fragment of an oil lamp, fragment of a pot, fragment of a vessel, fragment of a small bowl, fragment of a bowl, sherd of a jug.

Grave 113, cremation grave.

Finds: fragment of a bowl as an imitation of terra sigillata, sherd of bowl of terra sigillata.

Grave 114, cremation grave.

Finds: fragment of a painted vessel.

Grave 115, cremation grave.

Finds: iron nail, oil lamp, pl. V:15, fig. 75:6, fragment of a jug, fragment of a jug, fragment of a small bowl.

Grave 116, cremation grave.

Finds: fragments of a pot, fragment of a bowl.

Grave 117, cremation grave?

Finds: oil lamp, as pl. V:11, fig. 75:4, fragments of a small bowl.

Grave 118, cremation grave.

Finds: fragments of 3 jugs, as fig. 78:1.

Grave 119, skeleton grave of a man.

Finds: iron nails from boots.

Grave 120, cremation grave.

Finds: iron fittings of a chest, fragment of a small iron ring, iron hook, fragments of vessels (2).

Grave 121, cremation grave.

Finds: iron fittings, iron nail, oil lamp, as pl. V:14, fig. 75:21, folded beaker, fig. 77:9, fragment of a jug.

Grave 122, cremation grave?

Finds: sherds of a jug.

Grave 123, cremation grave.

Finds: iron fittings of a chest, iron nails (4), fragment of a jug, sherds of vessels (2).

Grave 124, cremation grave.

Finds: iron nails (8), iron nails from boots.

Grave 125, cremation grave.

Finds: iron nails from boots, iron nail, oil lamp, like pl. V:11, fig. 75:9.

Grave 126, cremation grave.

Finds: iron nails (3), iron nails from boots, sherds of a jug.

Grave 127, cremation grave.

Finds: fragments of a pot, fragment of a brick.

Grave 128, cremation grave.

Finds: sherd of a jug, fragment of a pot.

Grave 129, cremation grave.

Finds: oil lamp, as pl. V:16, fig. 75:2; fragment of an oil lamp, fig. 75:7, fragment of an oil lamp, fig. 75:26; fused glass beads, fragments of vessels (3), bowl, damaged.

Grave 130, grave?

Finds: sherds of a vessel.

Grave 131, cremation grave.

Finds: iron nails (3), iron nails from boots, sherds of a jug.

Grave 132, cremation grave.

Finds: iron nails from boots, fragment of an oil lamp, fig. 75:23, sherd of a vessel.

Grave 133, cremation grave.

Finds: fragment of a jug?

Grave 134, cremation grave.

Finds: fragment of a jug, fragments of glass.

Grave 135, skeleton grave, without finds.

Grave 136, cremation grave.

Finds: iron nails (3), jug, as fig. 78:1, sherds of vessels, iron slag.

Grave 137, cremation grave.

Finds: folded beaker, fig. 77:12.

Grave 138, cremation grave, bricks.

Finds: iron nail.

Grave 139, skeleton grave.

Finds: iron nails (4), iron nails from boots, jug, as fig. 80:5.

Grave 140, skeleton grave of a man.

Finds: clasp of bronze, small iron knife, coins: Constantine I (2), Crispus (1), jug, as fig. 78:8, fragment of a bowl.

Grave 141, cremation grave.

Finds: iron nails from boots, sherd of jug.

Grave 142, skeleton grave of a woman.

Finds: necklace of glass beads (179), fragment of a white metal ring, small jug, as fig. 78:7.

Grave 143, cremation grave.

Finds: iron nail, fragments of a pot.

Grave 144, skeleton grave of a man.

Finds: fibula of bronze, fig. 84:4, silver ring, fig. 74:8, coins: Constantine I, Constans, Constantius II, goblet of glass, fig. 73:7, small glass bottle, as fig. 72:10, iron buckle, pl. IV:2, iron point, pl. IV:15, iron knife, iron nails from boots, jug with lip, fig. 79:4, bowl, fig. 78:13.

Grave 145, skeleton grave.

Finds: fragment of an iron knife, iron nails (8).

Grave 146, cremation grave.

Finds: iron nails, iron nails from boots, iron fragment, oil lamp, as pl. V:16, fig. 75:16.

Graves 147-148, double skeleton grave.

Finds: iron clasp.

Grave 149, cremation grave.

Finds: small zoomorphic vessels of glass (2), oil lamp, as pl. V:16, fig. 75:4.

Grave 150, cremation grave.

Finds: fragment of a jug.

Grave 151, cremation grave.

Finds: iron nail, pot, fig. 77:11, sherd of a vessel.

Grave 152, cremation grave.

Finds: sherds of a vessel.

Grave 153, cremation grave.

Finds: iron nails (2), sherd of a bowl, sherd of a terra sigillata bowl.

Grave 154, cremation grave.

Finds: sherd of a jug.

Grave 155, cremation grave.

Finds: fragment of a vessel, sherd of a jug.

Grave 156, cremation grave.

Finds: oil lamp, pl. V:16, fig. 75:11, iron nail, fragment of a pot, fragment of a jug.

Grave 157, cremation grave.

Finds: iron nail, sherd of a vessel, fragment of a small glass vessel.

Grave 158, cremation grave.

Finds: sherds of a small vessel.

Grave 159, cremation grave.

Finds: small pot, fig. 77:6, sherd of a jug.

Grave 160, cremation grave.

Finds: jug, as fig. 78:2.

Grave 161, cremation grave.

Finds: fragment of a pot, sherd of a jug, sherd of a folded beaker.

Grave 162, cremation grave.

Finds: iron nails from boots, sherds of a jug.

Grave 163, cremation grave.

Finds: oil lamp, as pl. V:16, fig. 75:19, jug.

Grave 164, cremation grave.

Finds: oil lamp, as pl. V:11, iron nail, fragment of a jug.

Grave 165, cremation grave?

Finds: fragment of a jug, fragment of a vessel.

Grave 166, skeleton grave.

Finds: fragments of a small glass vessel.

Grave 167, skeleton grave of a man.

Finds: bronze fibula, fig. 84:4, small bronze ink pot, pl. VI:2, glass goblet (broken), jug with lip, fig. 81:11, fragment of a knife.

Damaged tombs of 1964

Finds: bronze fibula, fig. 84:5, jug, as fig. 79:2, jug with lip, fig. 81:14.

Finds from trial excavations: sherds of a censer, pl. VI:9, fragments of an oil lamp, enamelled statuette of a horse, pl. VI:8.

Note: the sexes of the skeletons have been determined anatomically.

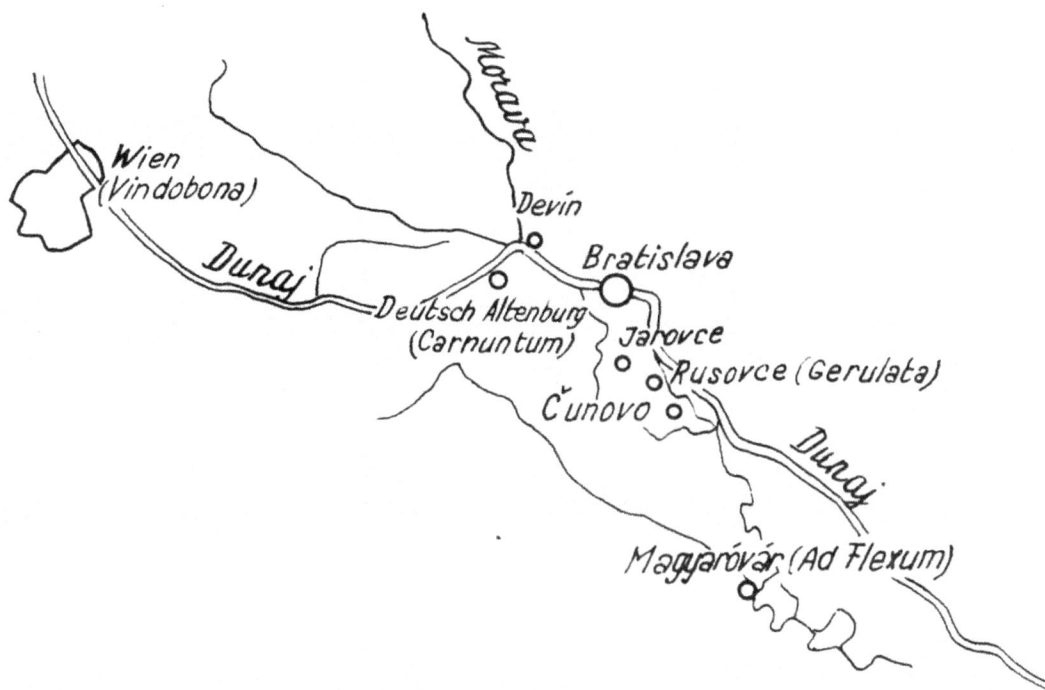

Fig. 1. Map: Location of Gerulata Rusovce

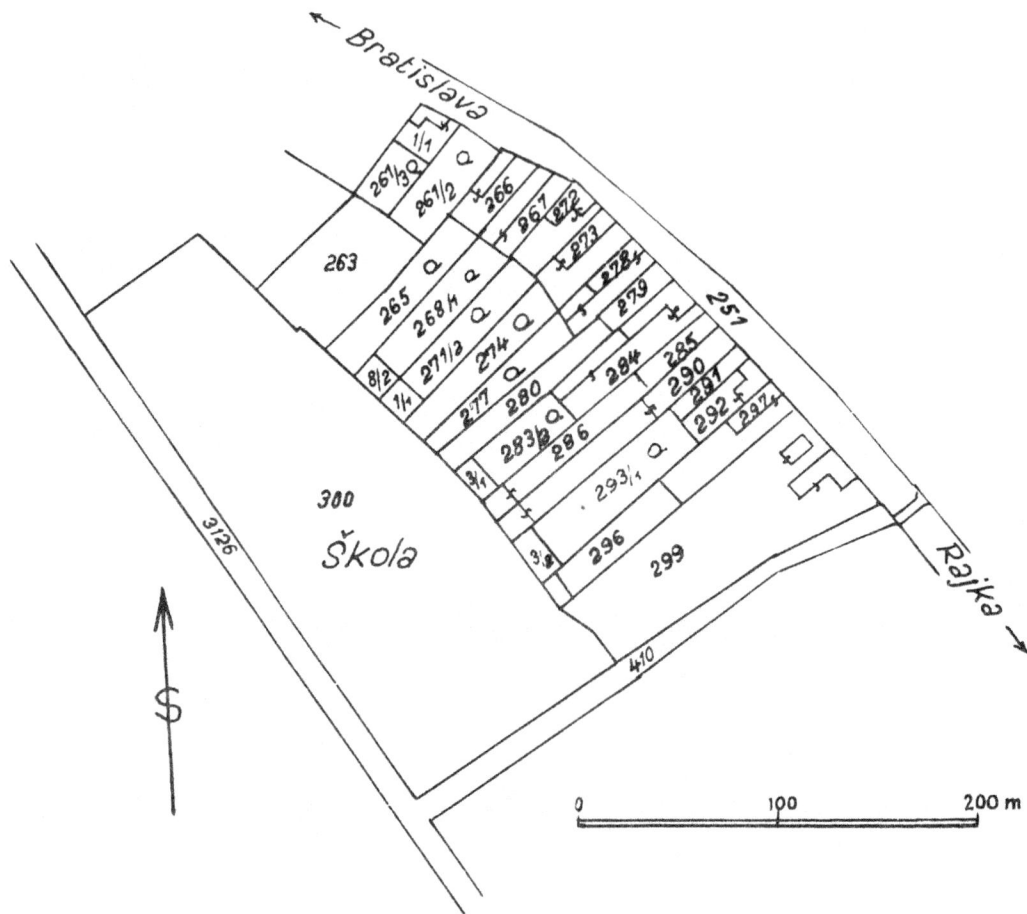

Fig. 2. Location of the cemetery

84

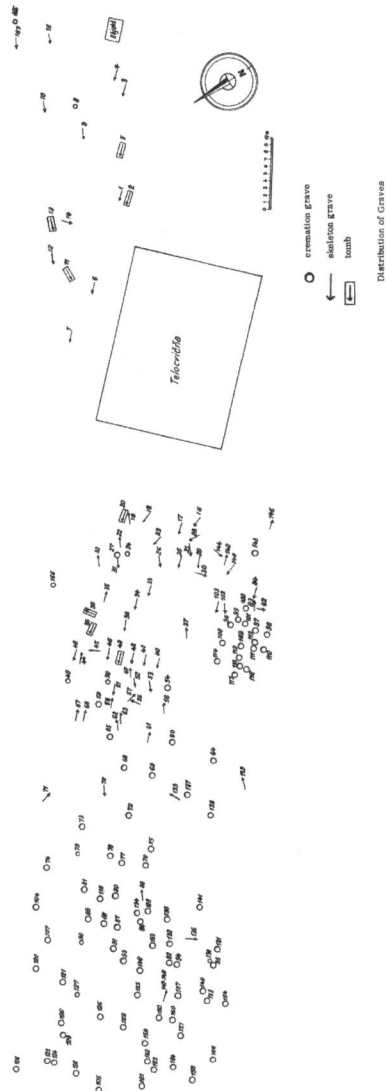

cremation grave
skeleton grave
tomb

Distribution of Graves

Telescrivitsia

Please note that a full-size version of this figure is available to download from www.barpublishing.com/additional-downloads.html. The original foldout has been reduced in size to match the A4 format of this book, the image is therefore not as clear as the original foldout. Please refer to the original foldout via the download for the original content.

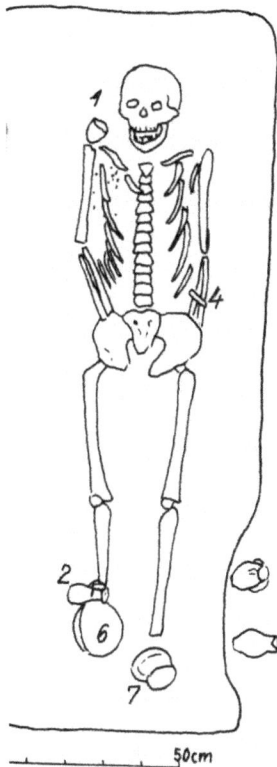

g. 3. Grave 1

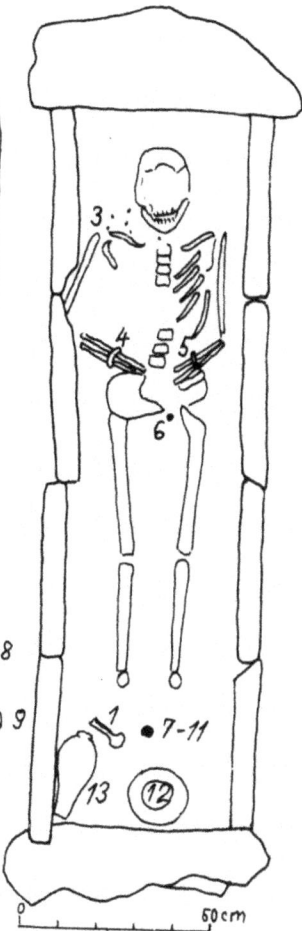

Fig. 4. Grave 2

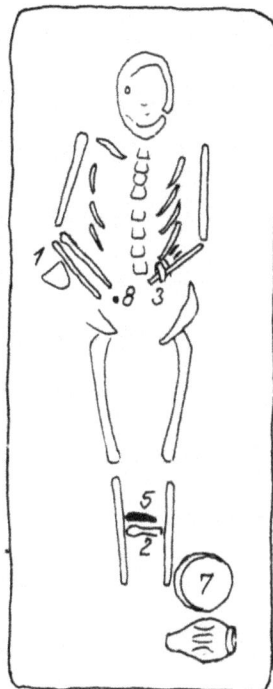

Fig. 5. Grave 3

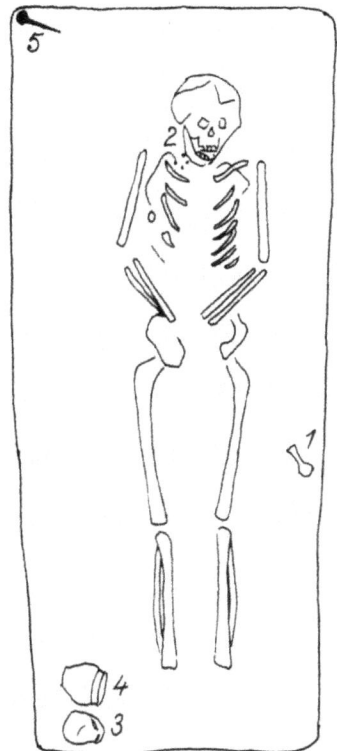

Fig. 6. Grave 4

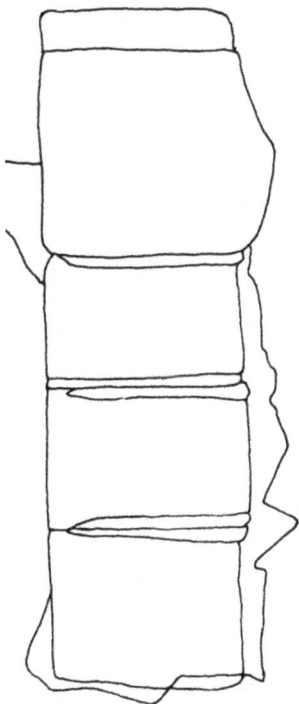

Fig. 7. Grave 5

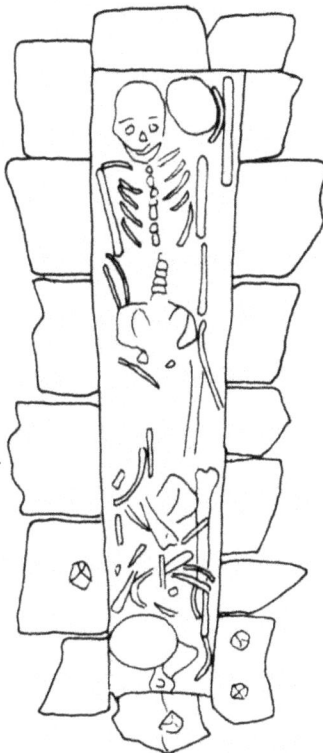

Fig. 8. Grave 5

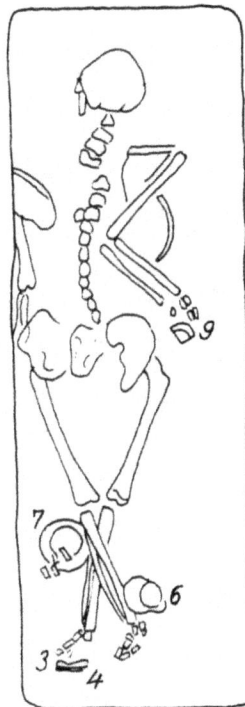

Fig. 9. Grave 7

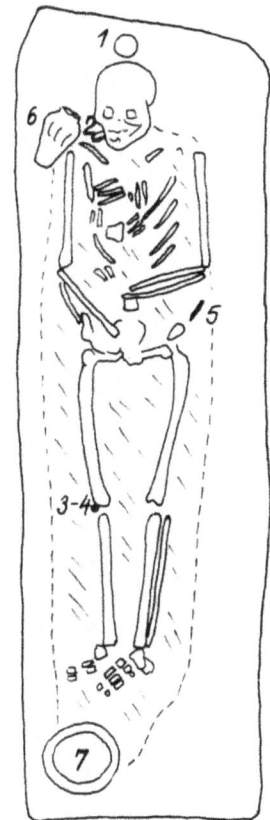

Fig. 10. Grave 9

85

Grave 11

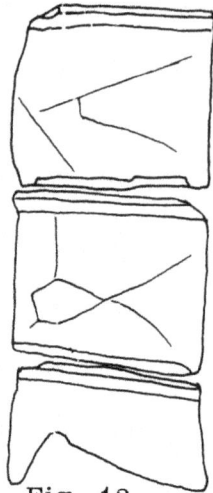

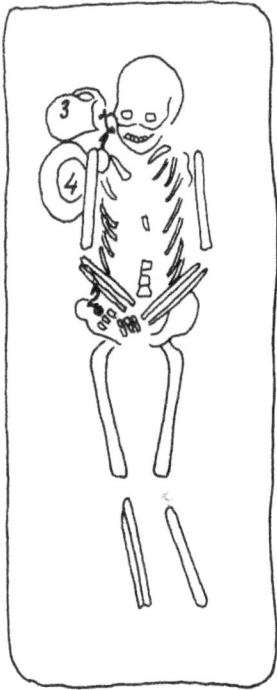

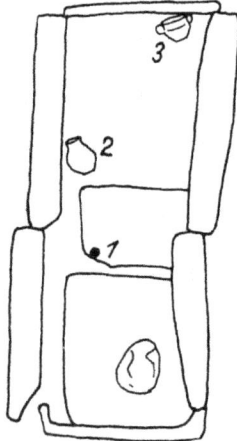

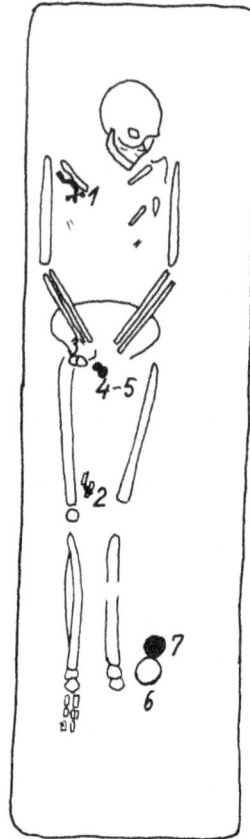

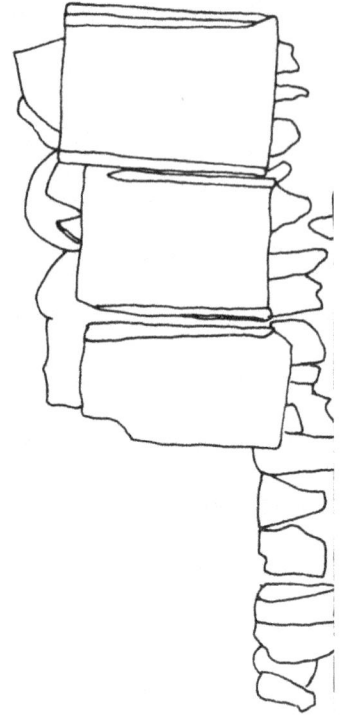

Fig. 12.

Fig. 11.   Grave 10

Fig. 13.

Fig. 14.   Grave 12

Fig. 15.   Grave 13

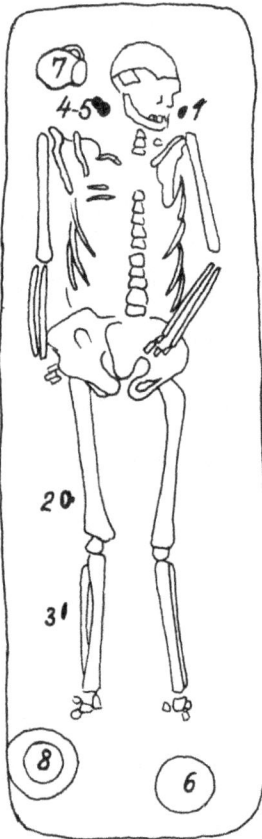

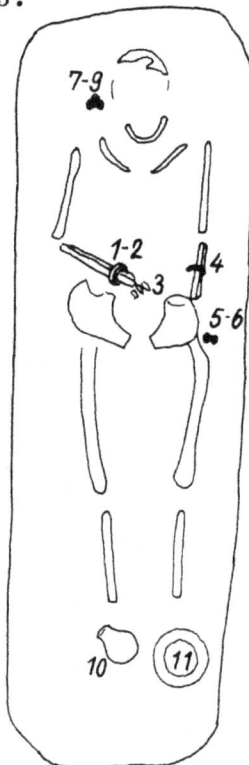

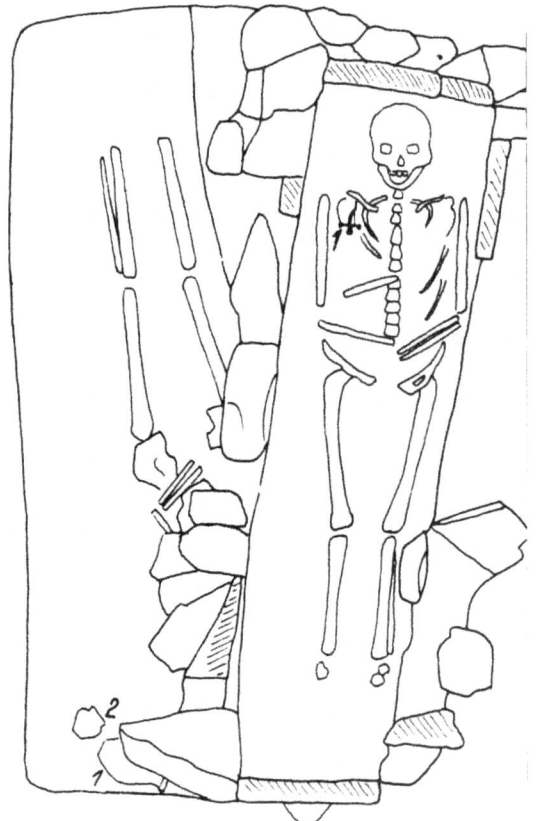

Fig. 17.   Grave 18

Fig. 16.   Grave 14

Fig. 18.   Graves 19 and 20

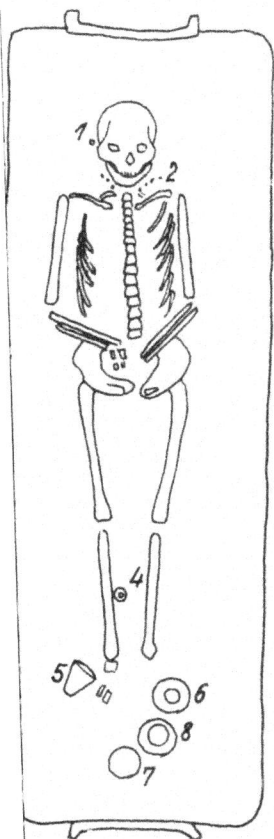

Fig. 19.　Grave 21

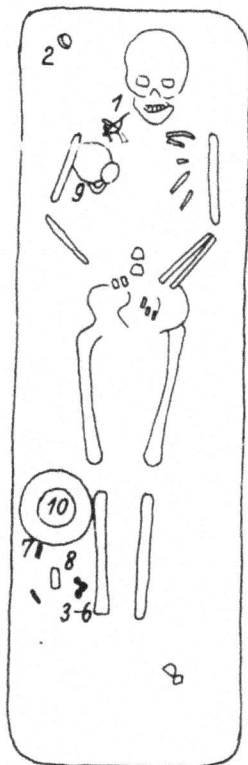

Fig. 20.　Grave 25

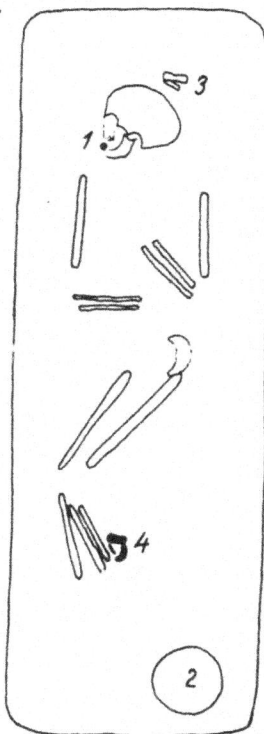

Fig. 21.　Grave 28

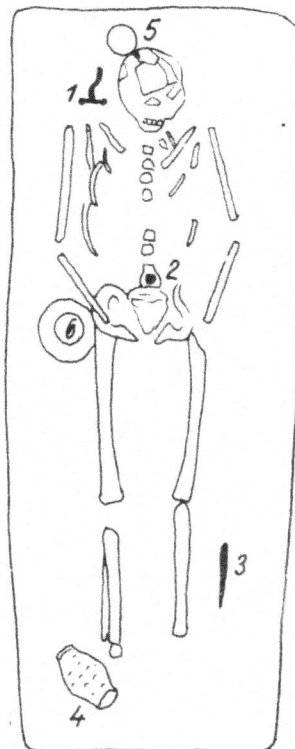

Fig. 22.　Grave 29

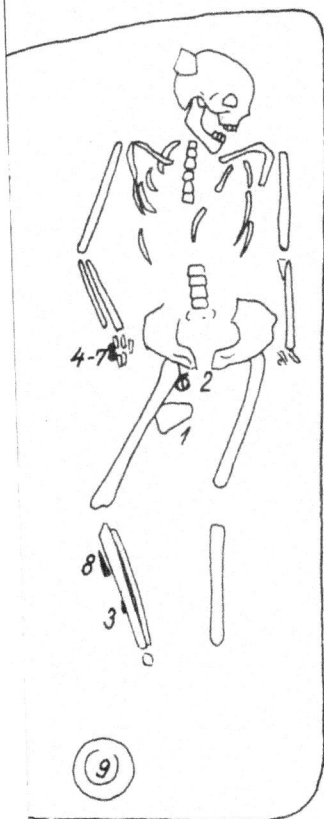

Fig. 23.　Grave 30

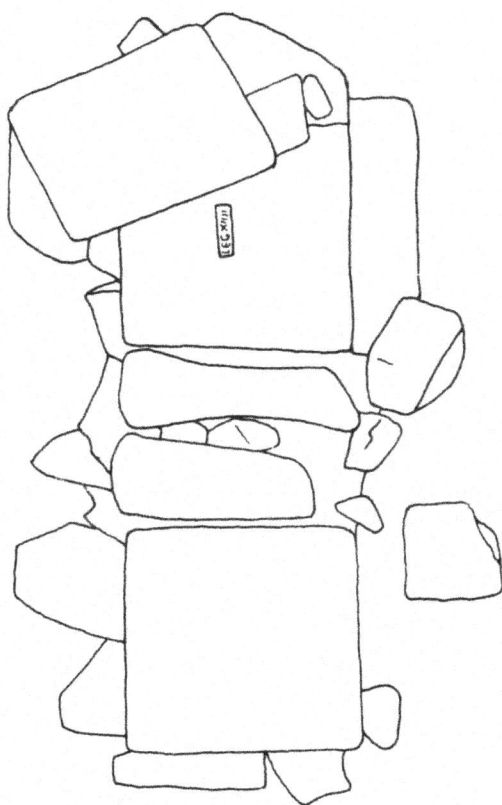

Fig. 24.　Grave 36

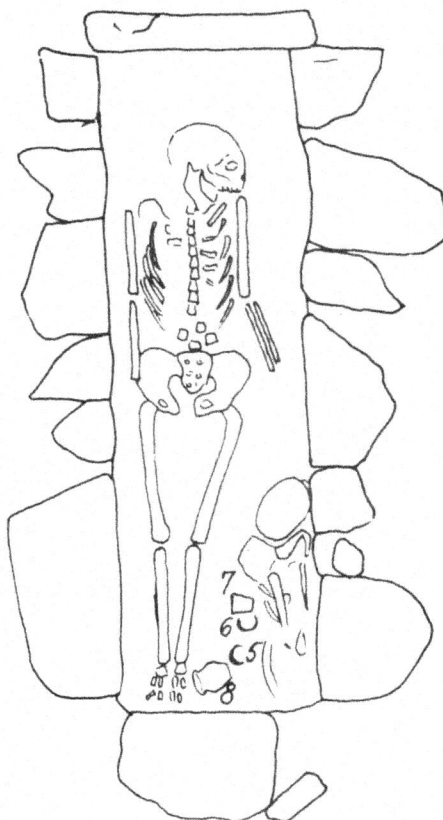

Fig. 25.　Grave 36

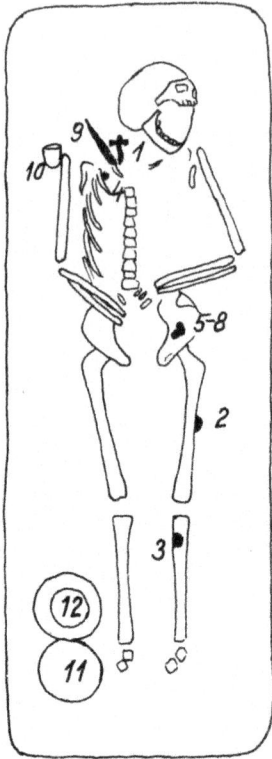

Fig. 26. Grave 32

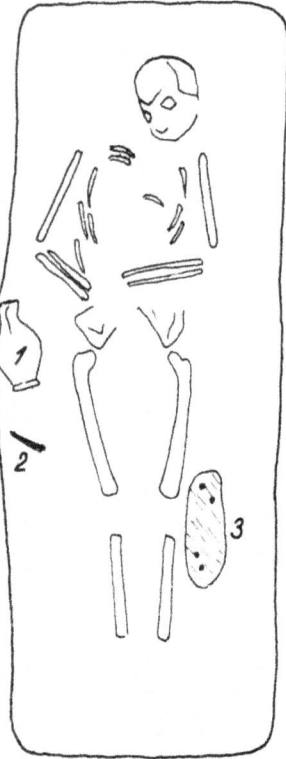

Fig. 27. Grave 37

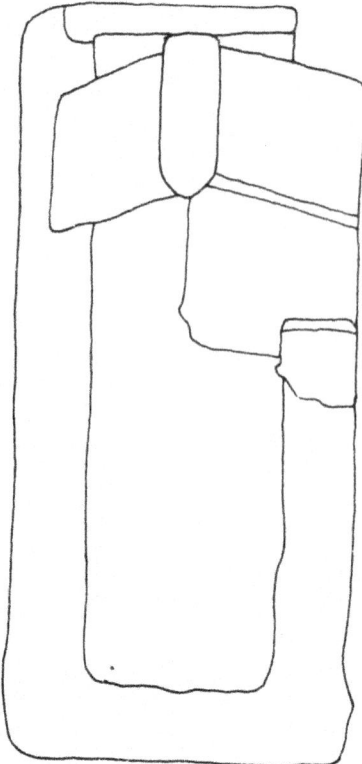

Fig. 28. Grave 39

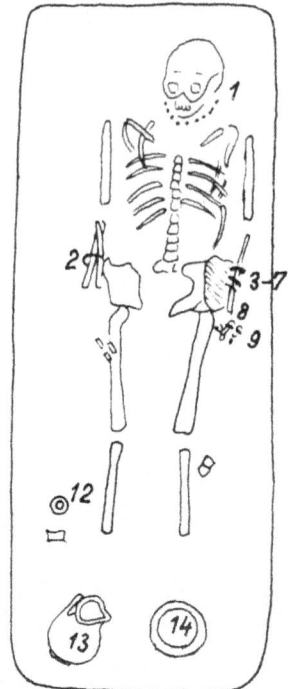

Fig. 29. Grave 41

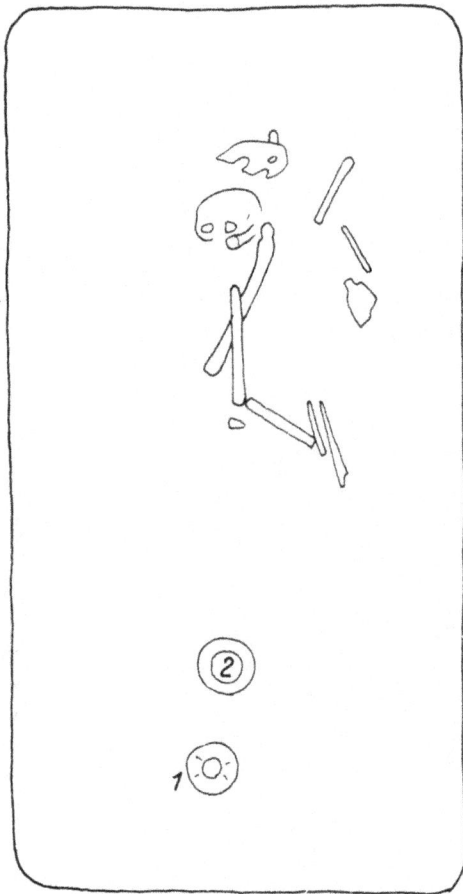

Fig. 30. Grave 42

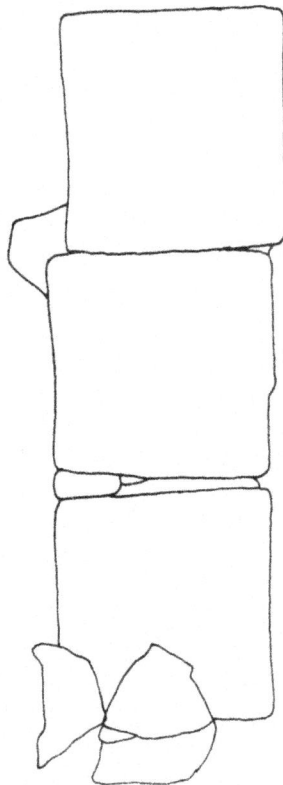

Fig. 31. Grave 43

Fig. 32. Grave 43

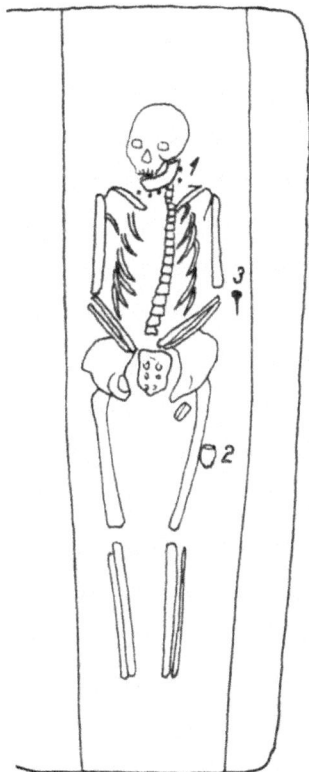

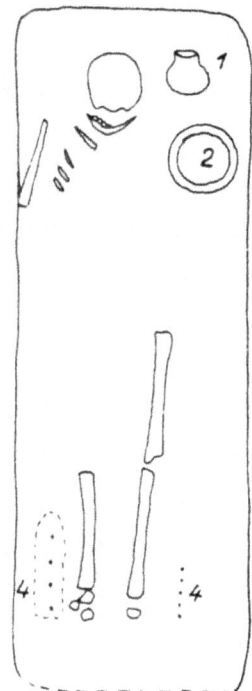

Fig. 33. Grave 51   Fig. 34. Grave 52   Fig. 35. Grave 53   Fig. 40. Grave 67

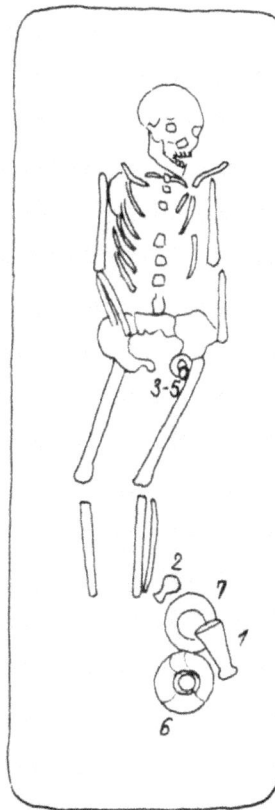

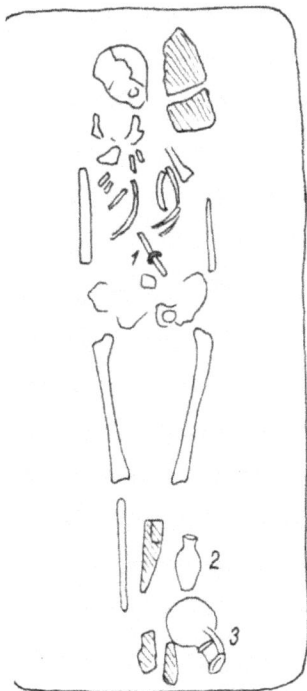

Fig. 36. Grave 55   Fig. 37. Grave 56   Fig. 38. Grave 59   Fig. 39. Grave 63

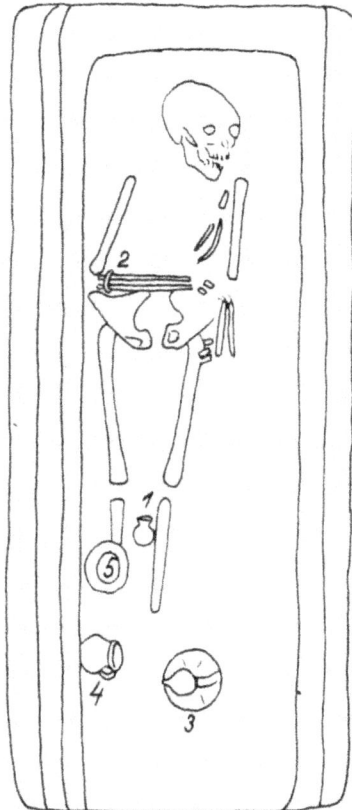

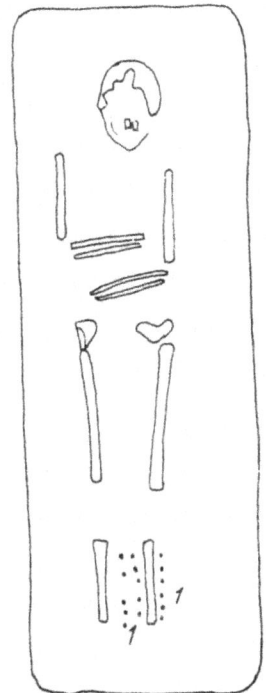

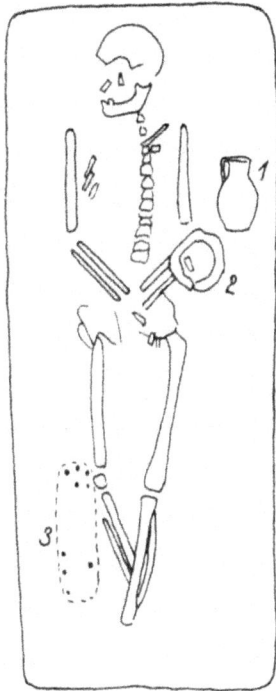

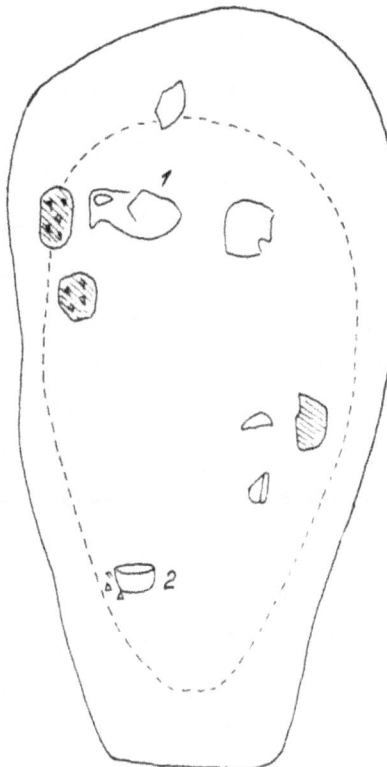

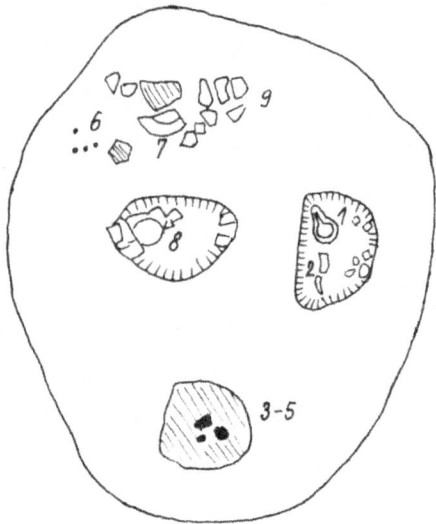

Fig. 41. Grave 68

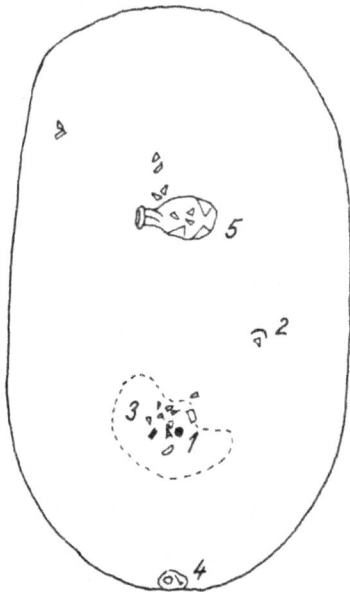

Grave 73

Fig. 43.

Fig. 42. Grave 72

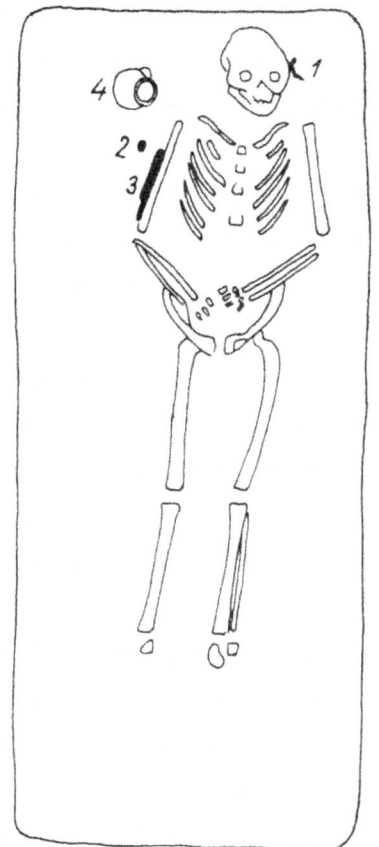

Fig. 44. Grave 74

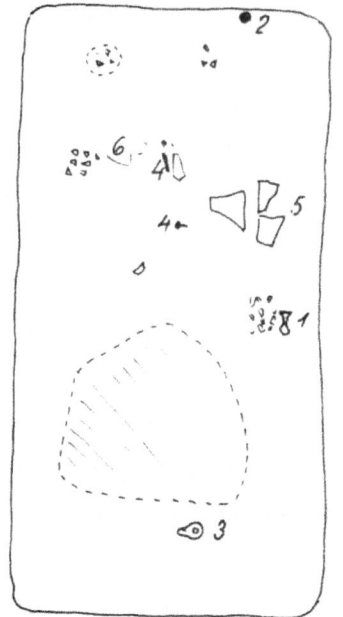

Fig. 45. Grave 81

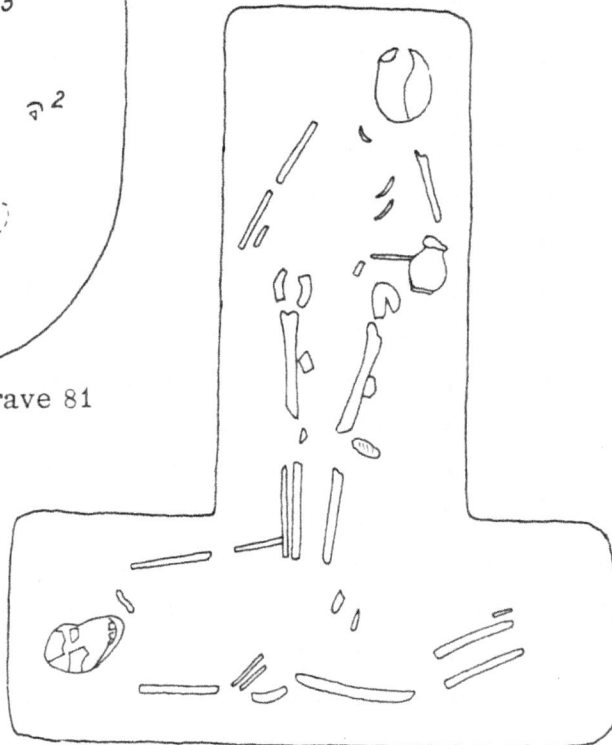

Fig. 46. Graves 82 and 83

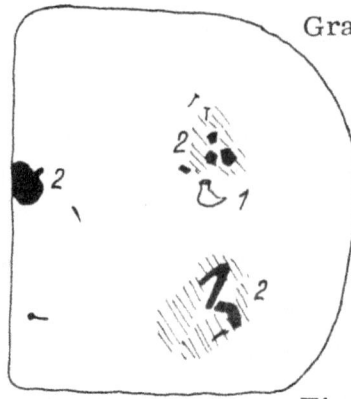

Fig. 47. Grave 84

Grave 87

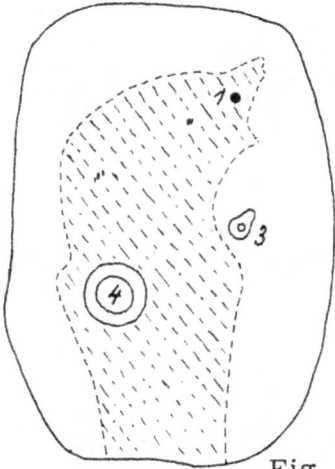

Fig. 48.

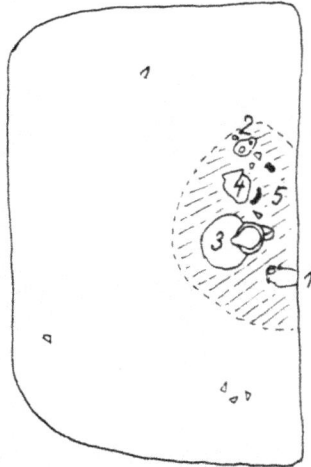

Fig. 52. Grave 99

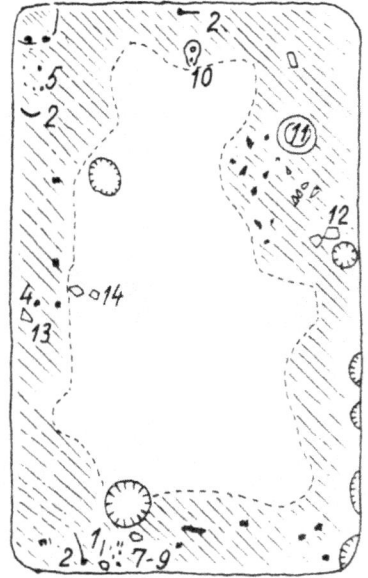

0   100 cm

Fig. 49. Grave 94

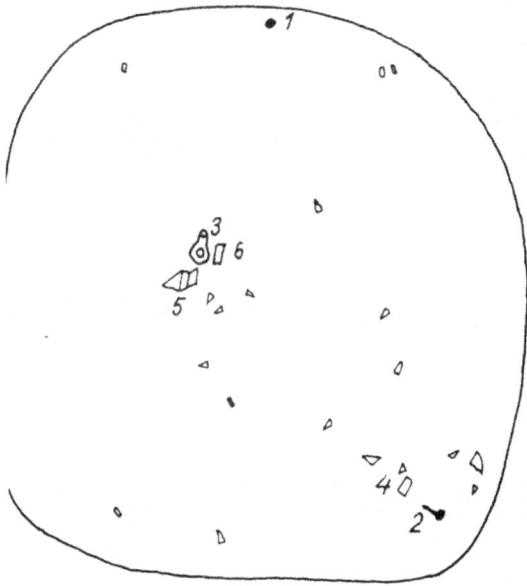

0   50 cm

Fig. 50. Grave 97

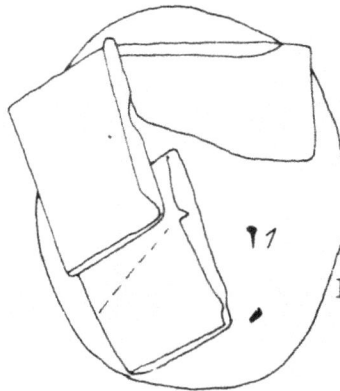

Fig. 53. Grave 101

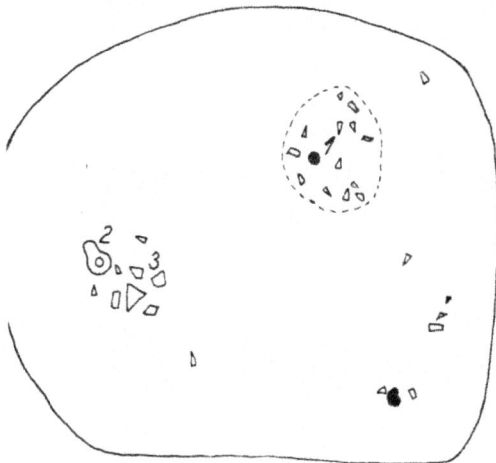

Fig. 51. Grave 98

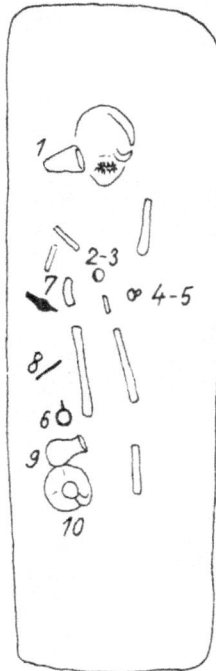

Fig. 54. Grave 102

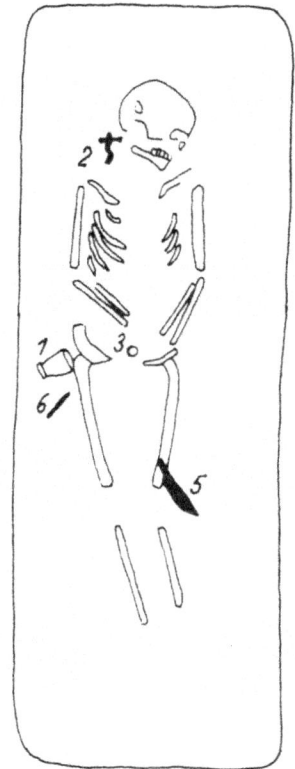

Fig. 55. Grave 103

91

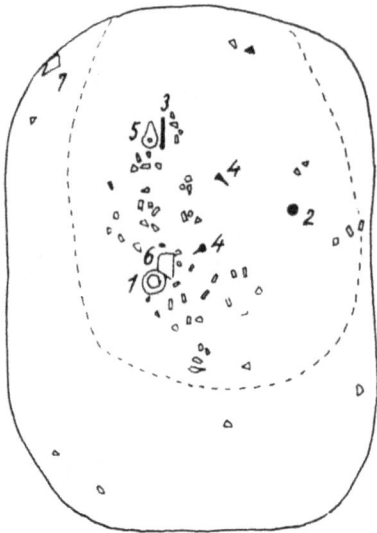

Fig. 56.   Grave 105

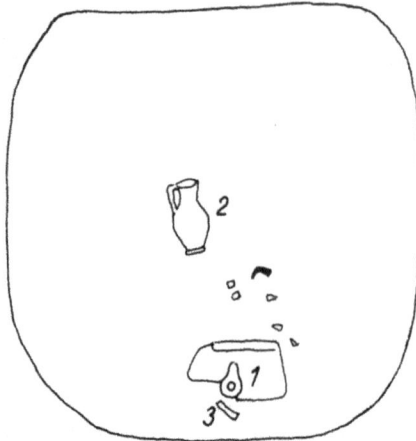

Fig. 57.   Grave 110

Fig. 58.   Grave 115.

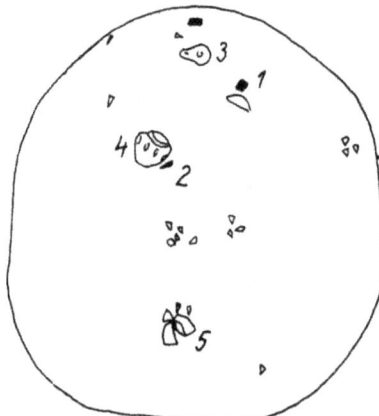

Fig. 59.   Grave 121

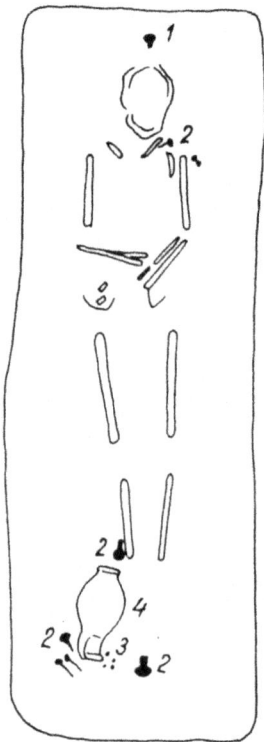

Fig. 61.   Grave 139

Fig. 60.   Grave 136

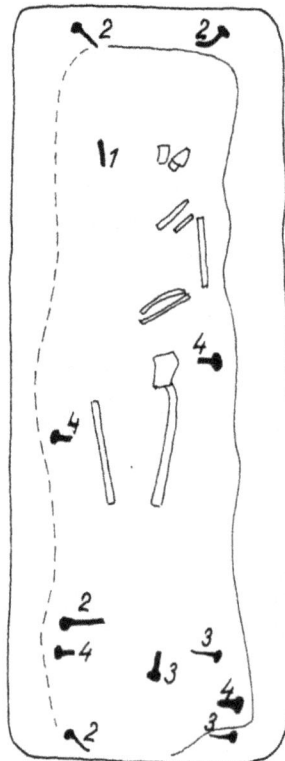

Fig. 63.   Grave 145

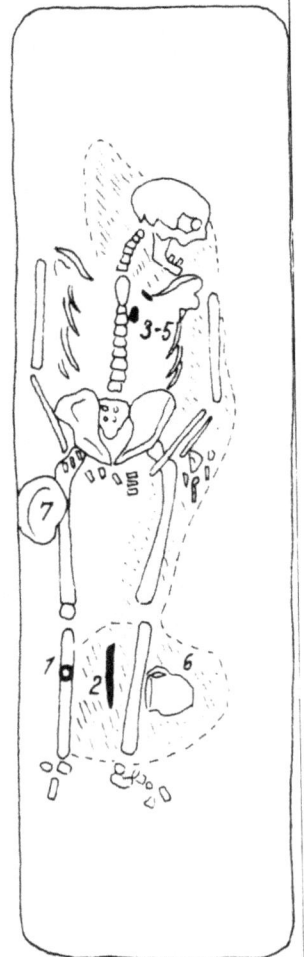

Fig. 62.   Grave 14(

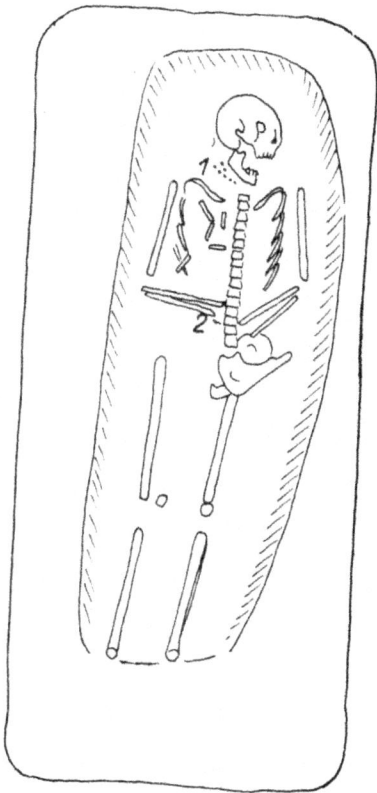

Fig. 65. Grave 142

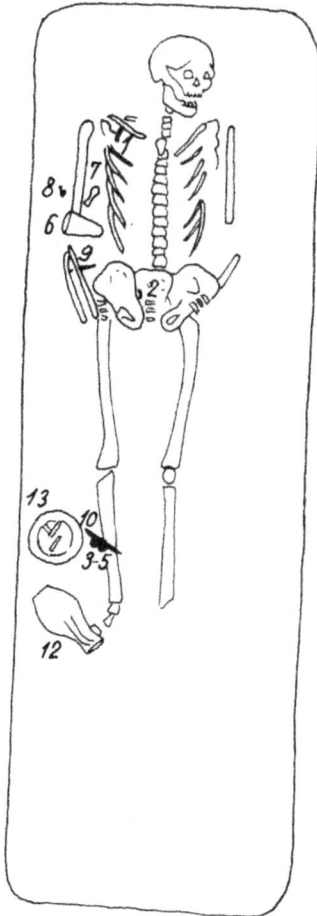

Fig. 66. Grave 146

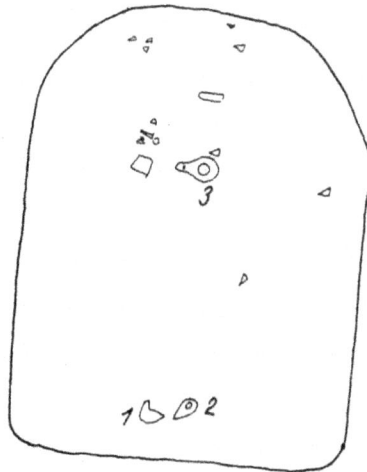

Fig. 64. Grave 144

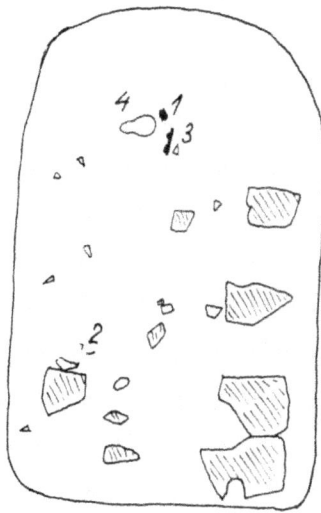

Fig. 67.
Graves
147 and
148

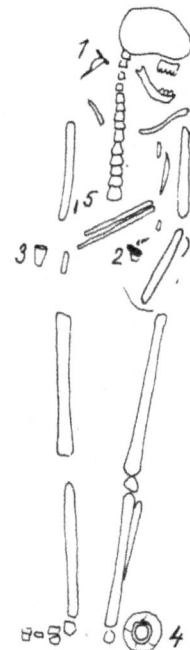

Fig. 68. Grave 149

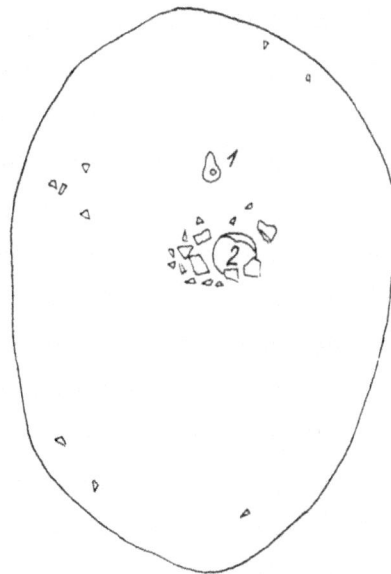

Fig. 69. Grave 163

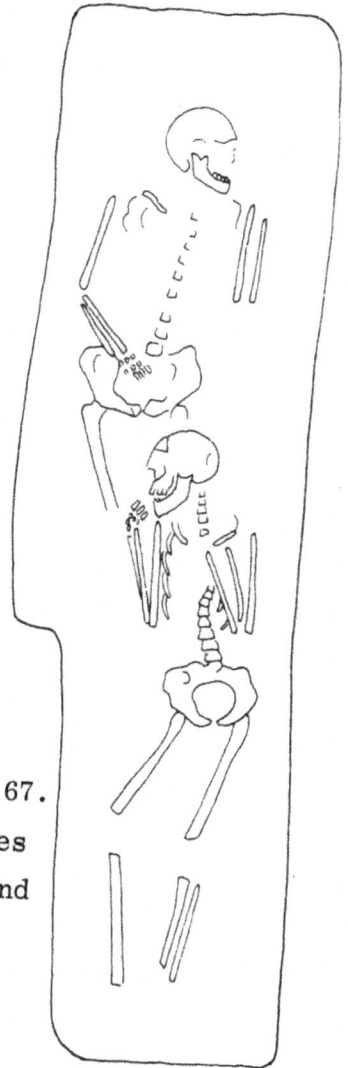

Fig. 70. Grave 167

93

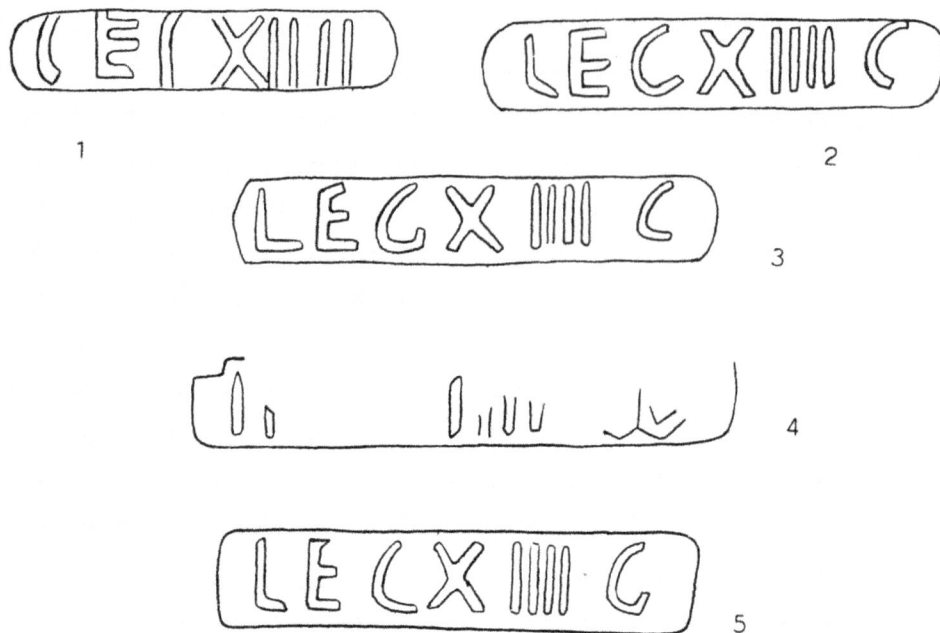

Fig. 71. Stamps on bricks: 1-grave 6; 2-4-grave 36; 5-grave 43.
Scale 1:2

94

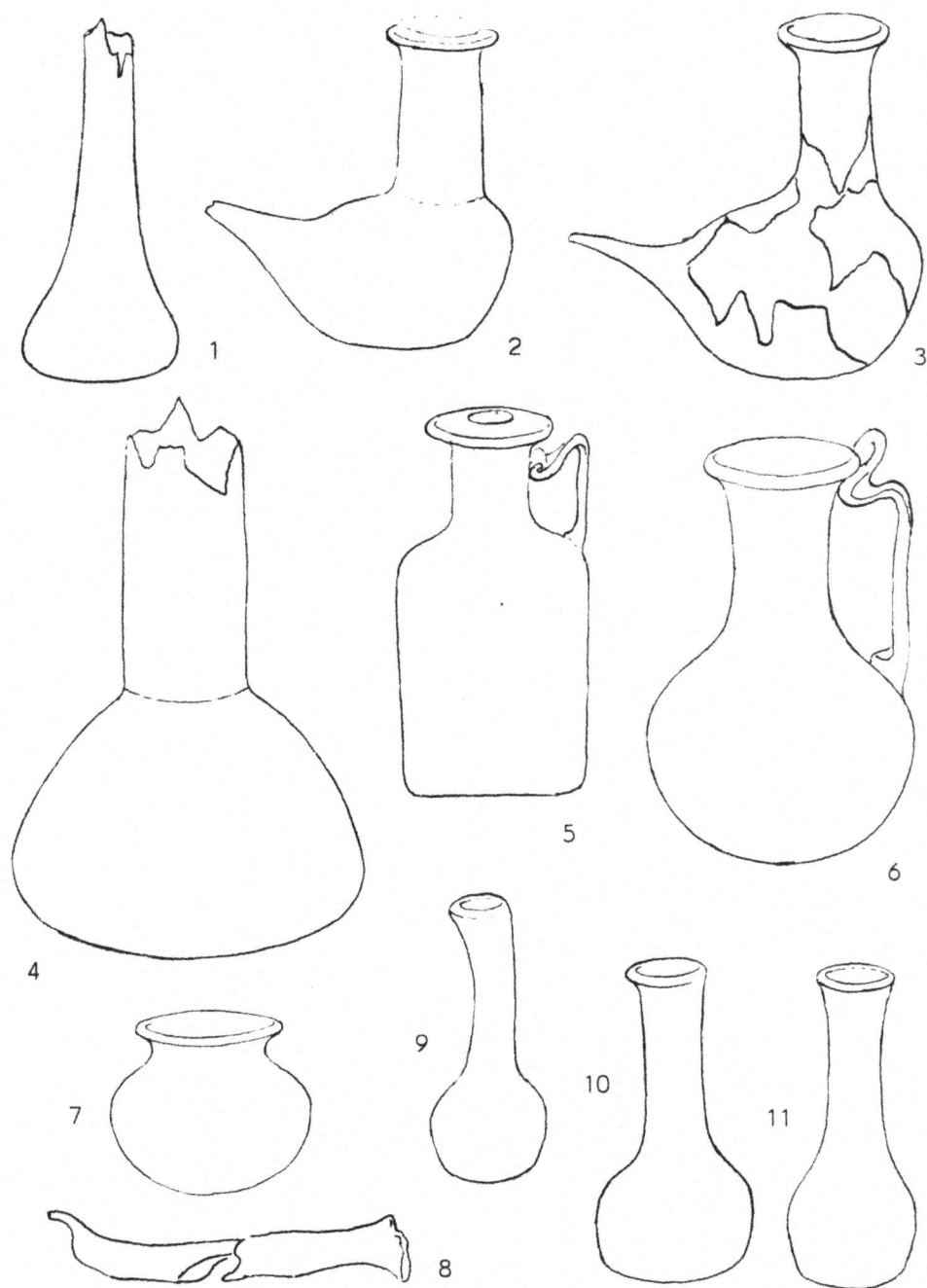

Fig. 72. Glass vessels from cremation graves: 1-unguentarium, grave 72;
2, 3-zoomorphic vessels, graves 73, 149; 4-5-bottle, grave 92, 99;
6-small jug, grave 65; 7-small vessel, grave 105; 8-unguentarium,
grave 68. Glass from the skeleton graves: 9-11-unguentaria,
graves 3, 53, 2. Scale 1:2

Fig. 73. Glass vessels from the skeleton graves: 1, 2-unguentaria, graves
2, 4; 3, 4-cylindrical goblets, graves 1, 3; 5-cup, grave 15;
6-8-conical goblets, graves 102, 144, 9. Scale 1:2

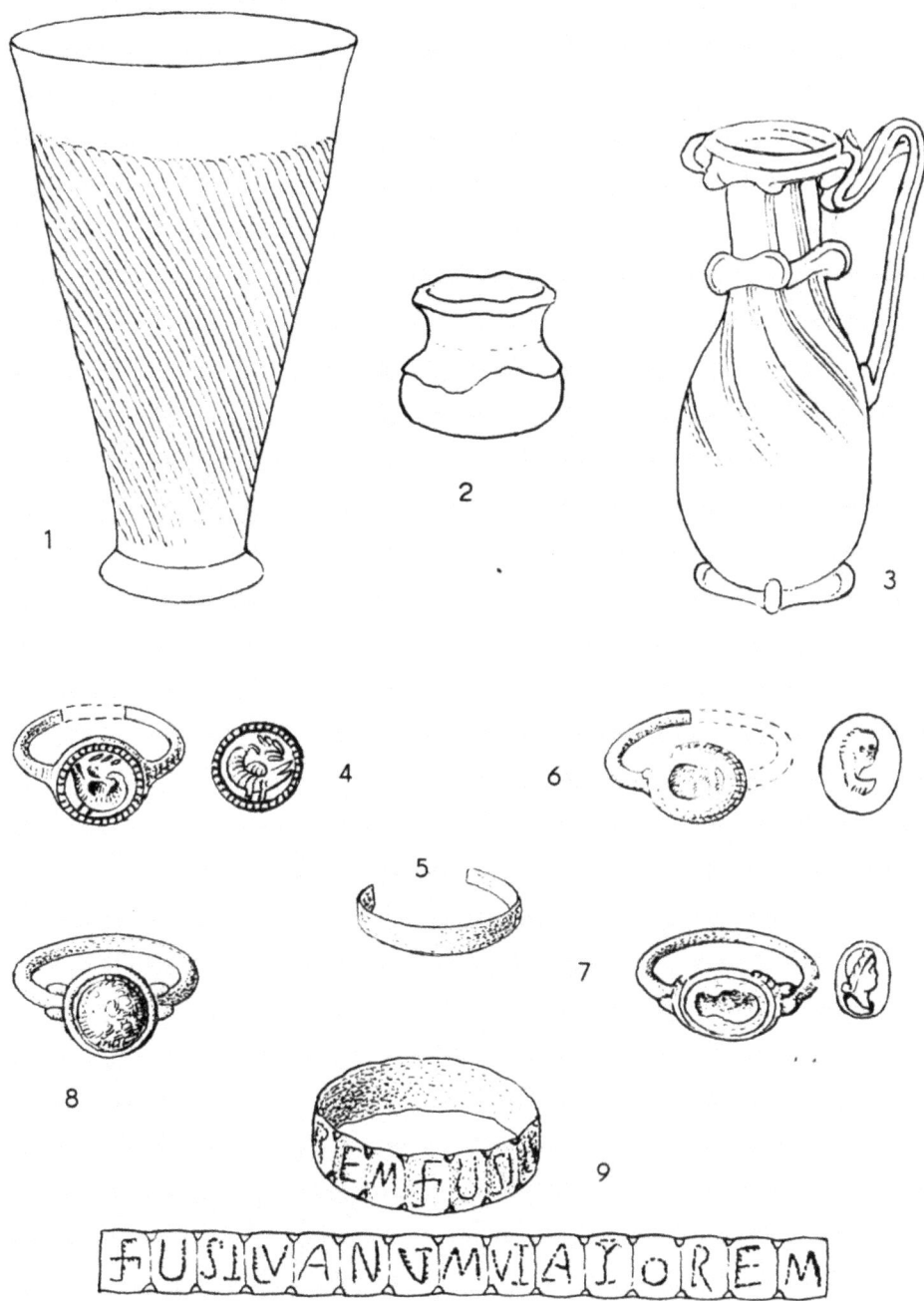

Fig. 74. Glass from the skeleton graves: 1-conical goblet, grave 53; 2-small vessel, grave 36; 3-small jug, grave 1. Scale 1:2.
Ornaments from the skeleton graves: 4-grave 12; 5,7-grave 41; 6-grave 14; 8-grave 144; 9-grave 25. Scale 1:1

Fig. 75. Stamps on oil lamps: 1-AGILIS F, grave 87; 2-CPSF, grave 129; 3,4-FESTI, graves 81, 117; 5-17-FORTIS, graves 110,115, 129, 149, 125, 75, 156, 103, 66, 60, 74, 146, 69; 18-LNARI, grave 94; 19-PULLI, grave 163; 20-SCA, grave 97; 21, 22- VIBIUS, grave 121, 99; 23-IER, grave 132; 24-NR, grave 108; 25-uncertain, grave 80; 26-cursive script, grave 129. Scale 1:1

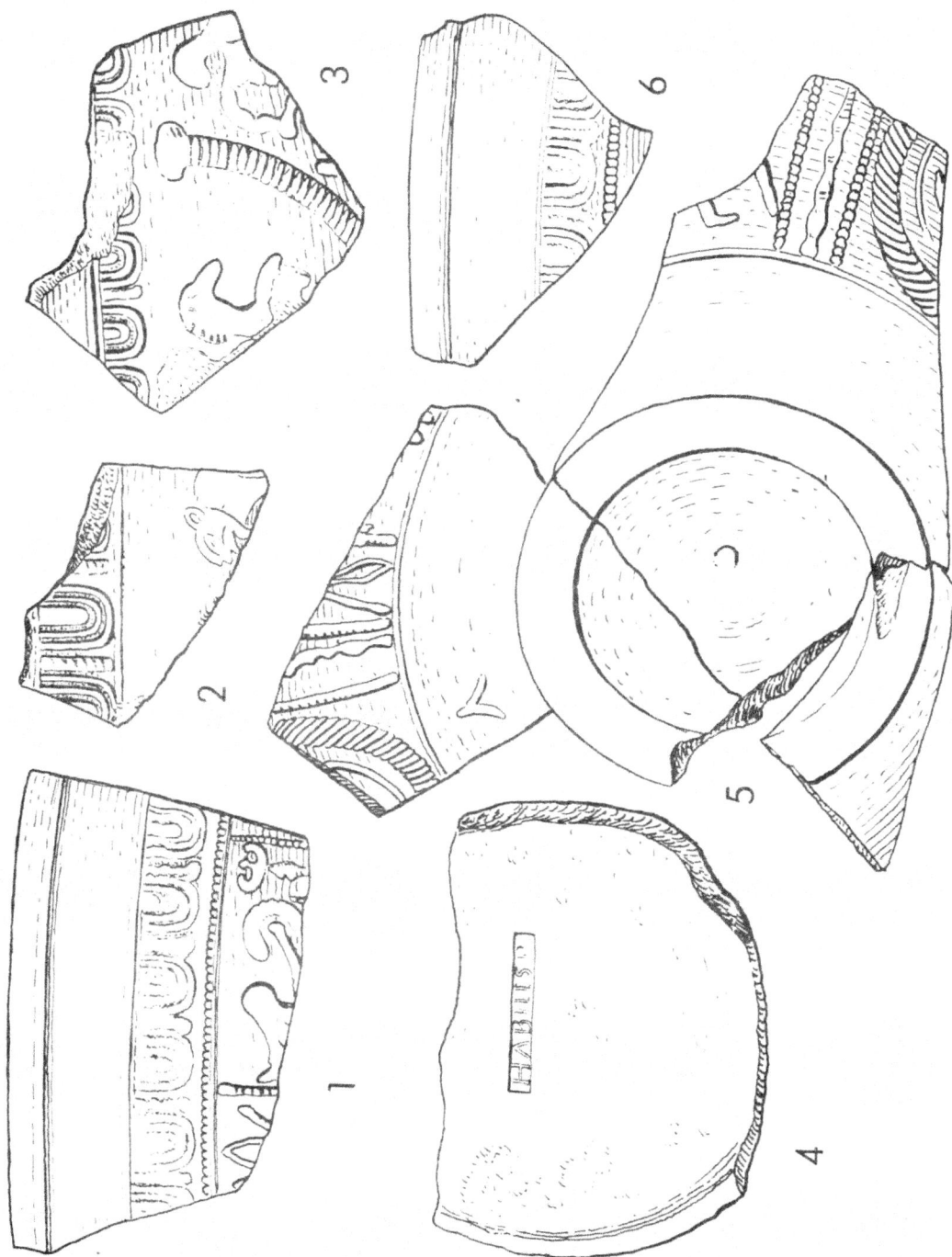

Fig. 76. Terra sigillata. 1,3-6 unstratified sherds, 2-grave 7. Scale 2:3

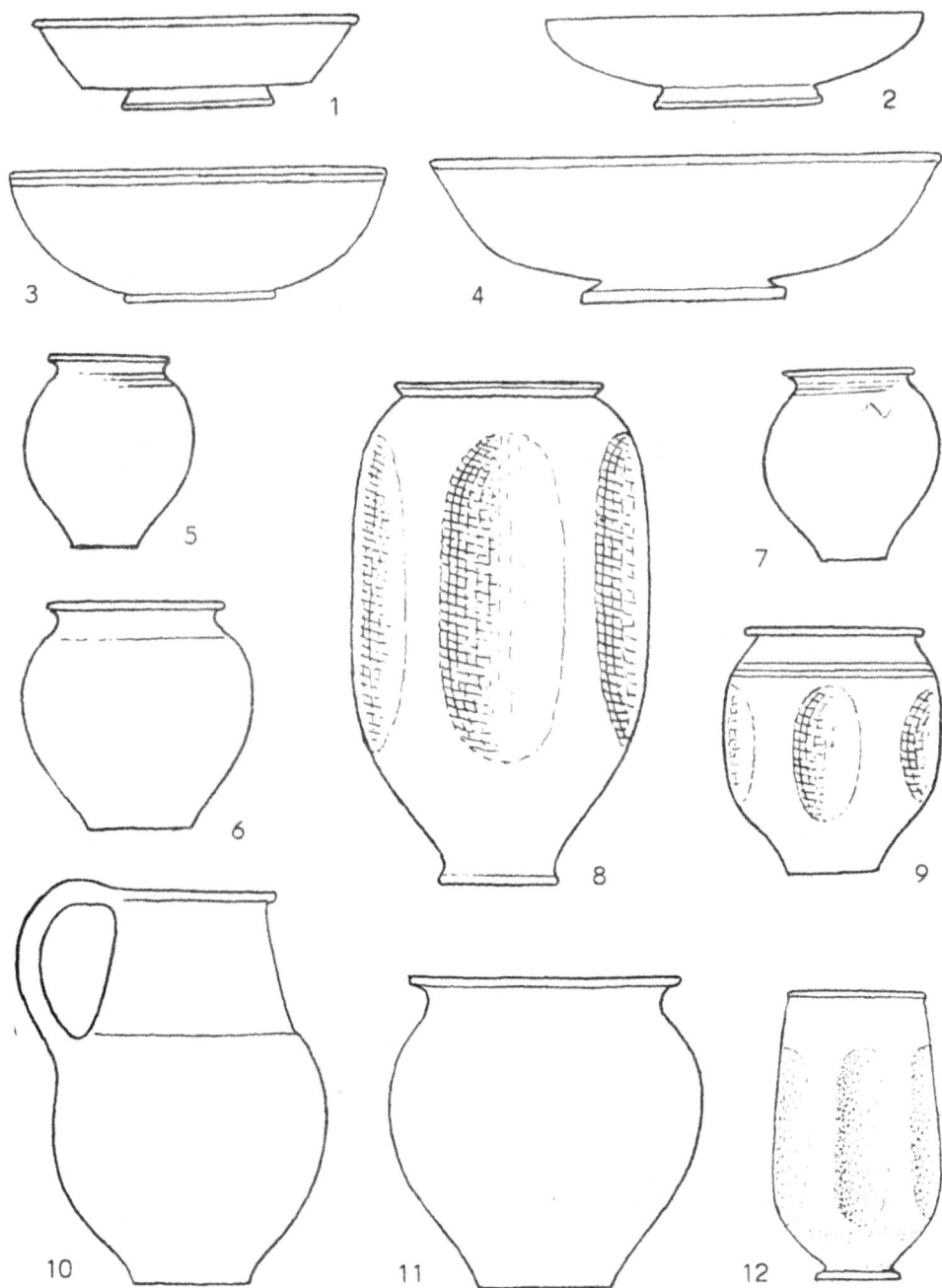

Fig. 77. Types of vessels from the cremation graves. Terra sigillata: 1,2-
dish, graves 87, 65; imitation terra sigillata: 3,4-dish, grave 78,
90; rough grey pottery: 5-7-small pot, graves 54, 159, 99; 8,9-
folded beaker, graves 65, 121; 10-jug with lip, grave 99: 11-pot,
grave 151; painted ceramic: 12-folded beaker, grave 137.
Scale 1:4

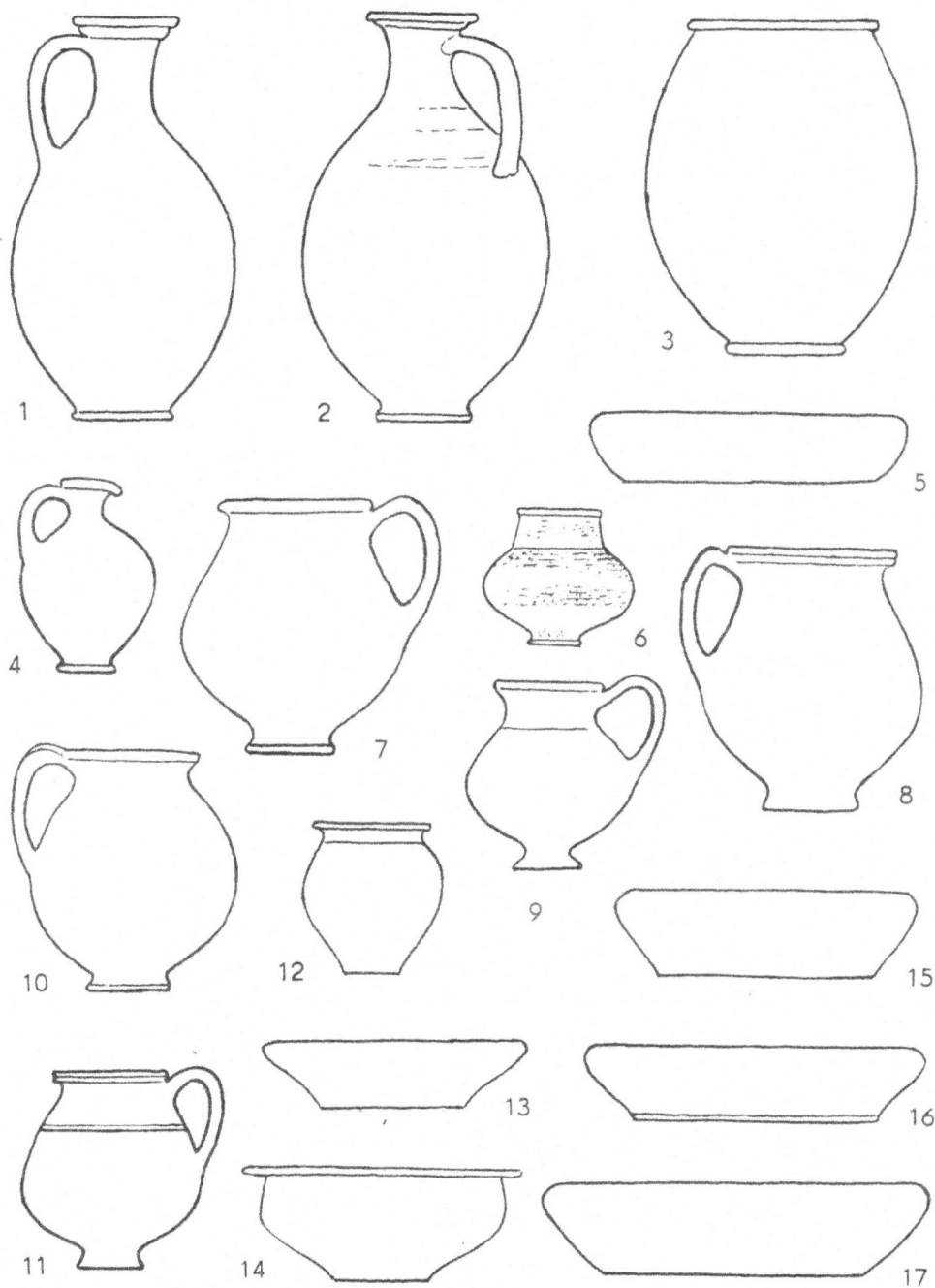

Fig. 78. Types of vessels from the cremation graves. Yellow ceramic:
1,2-jug, graves 74, 110; 3-vessel, grave 92; 4-small jug, grave
109; rough ceramic: 5-bowl, grave 94; fine ceramic: 6-small
vessel, grave 65. Types of vessels from the skeleton graves.
Grey rough ceramic: 7-11-small jug, graves 8, 1, 4, 84, 18;
12-small pot, grave 47; 13-17-bowl, graves 144, 56, 29, 18, 63.
Scale 1:4

Fig. 79.   Types of vessels from the skeleton graves.   Grey rough ceramic:
1-folded beaker, grave 3; 2,6-jugs, graves 6, 53; 3-small vessel,
grave 11; 4,5-jugs with lips, graves 144, 70; polished ceramic:
7,9-jugs, graves 17, 102; 8-dish, grave 14; painted ceramic:
10-dish, grave 25.   Scale 1:4

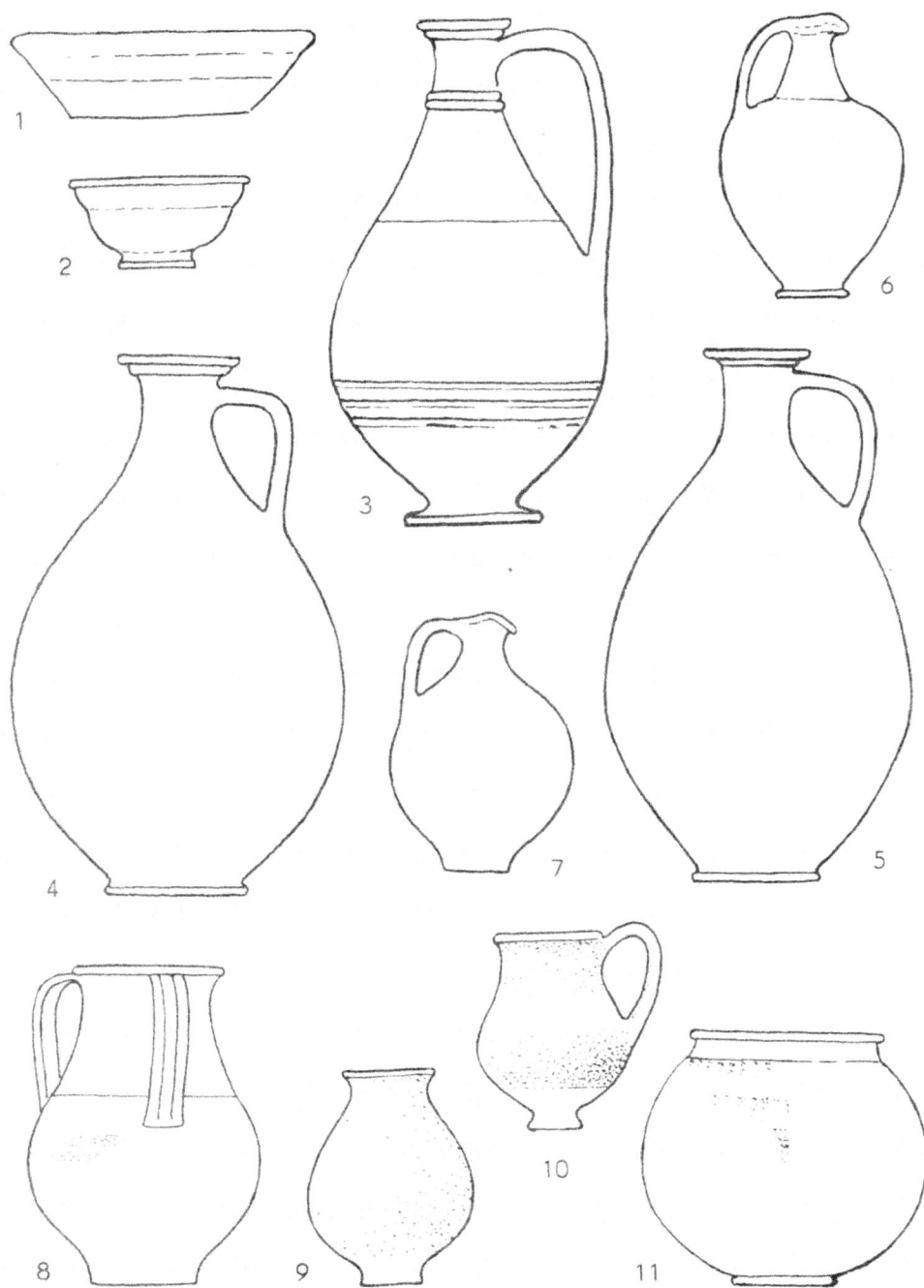

Fig. 80.   Types of vessels from the skeleton graves.   Polished ceramic:
1,2-dishes, graves 30, 19;   yellow ceramic: 3-5,jugs, graves 2,
28, 19;   6,7-small jugs with lips, graves 15, 47;   painted ceramic:
8-amphora, grave 34;   9-small vase, grave 1;   10-small jug, grave
31;   11-vase, grave 71.   Scale 1:4

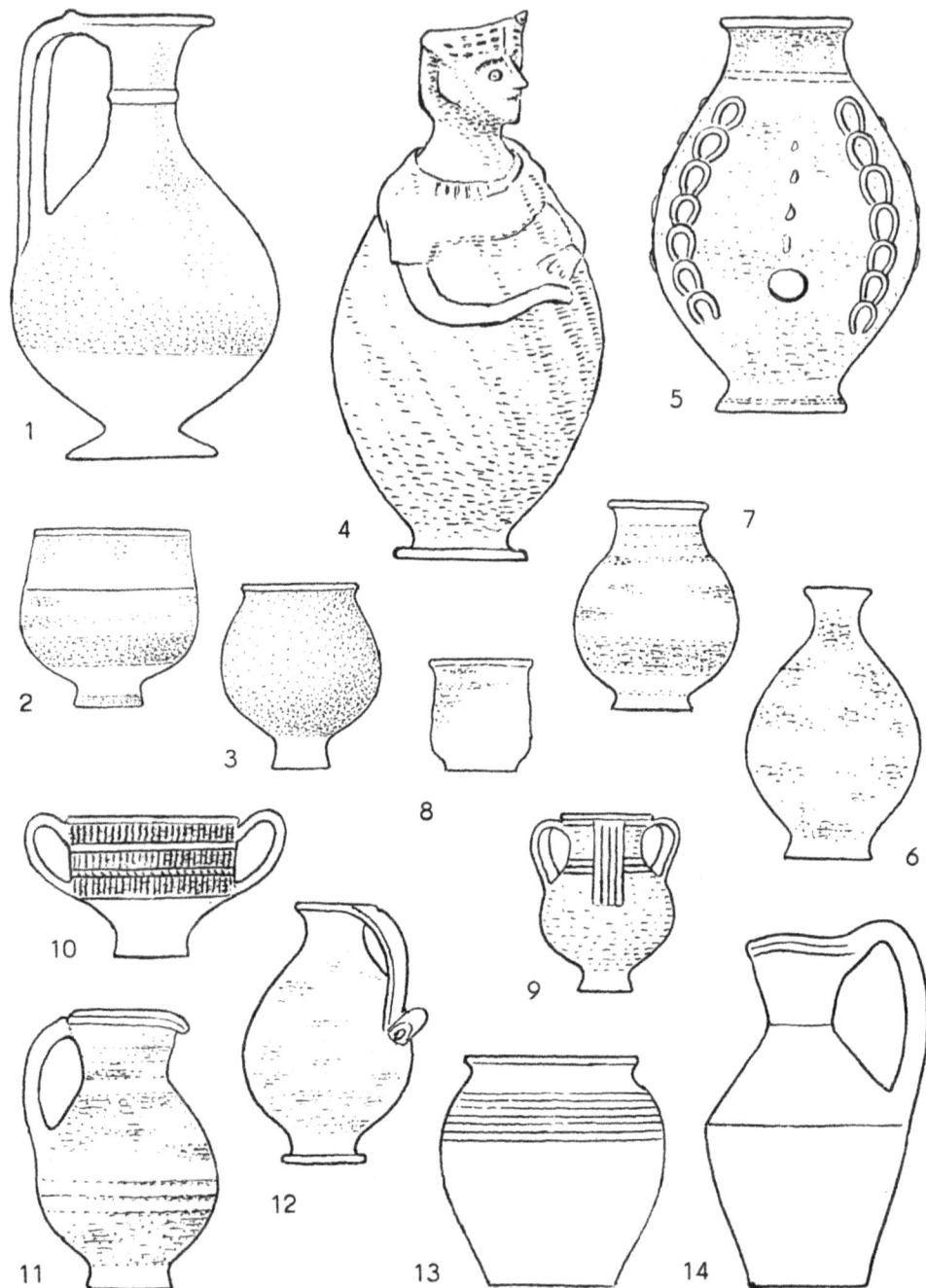

Fig. 81. Types of vessels from the skeleton graves. Painted ceramic:
1-jug, grave 55; 2,3-goblets, graves 70, 29; glazed ceramic:
4-anthropomorphic vessel, grave 18; 5-vase, grave 29; 6,7-
small vases, graves 55, 102; 8-small goblet, grave 36; 9-ampho
grave 1; 10-cup, grave 11, 11-jug with lip, grave 167; 12-small
jug, grave 21; domestic ceramic: 13-pot, grave 4; 14-jug with
lip, damaged grave. Scale 1:4

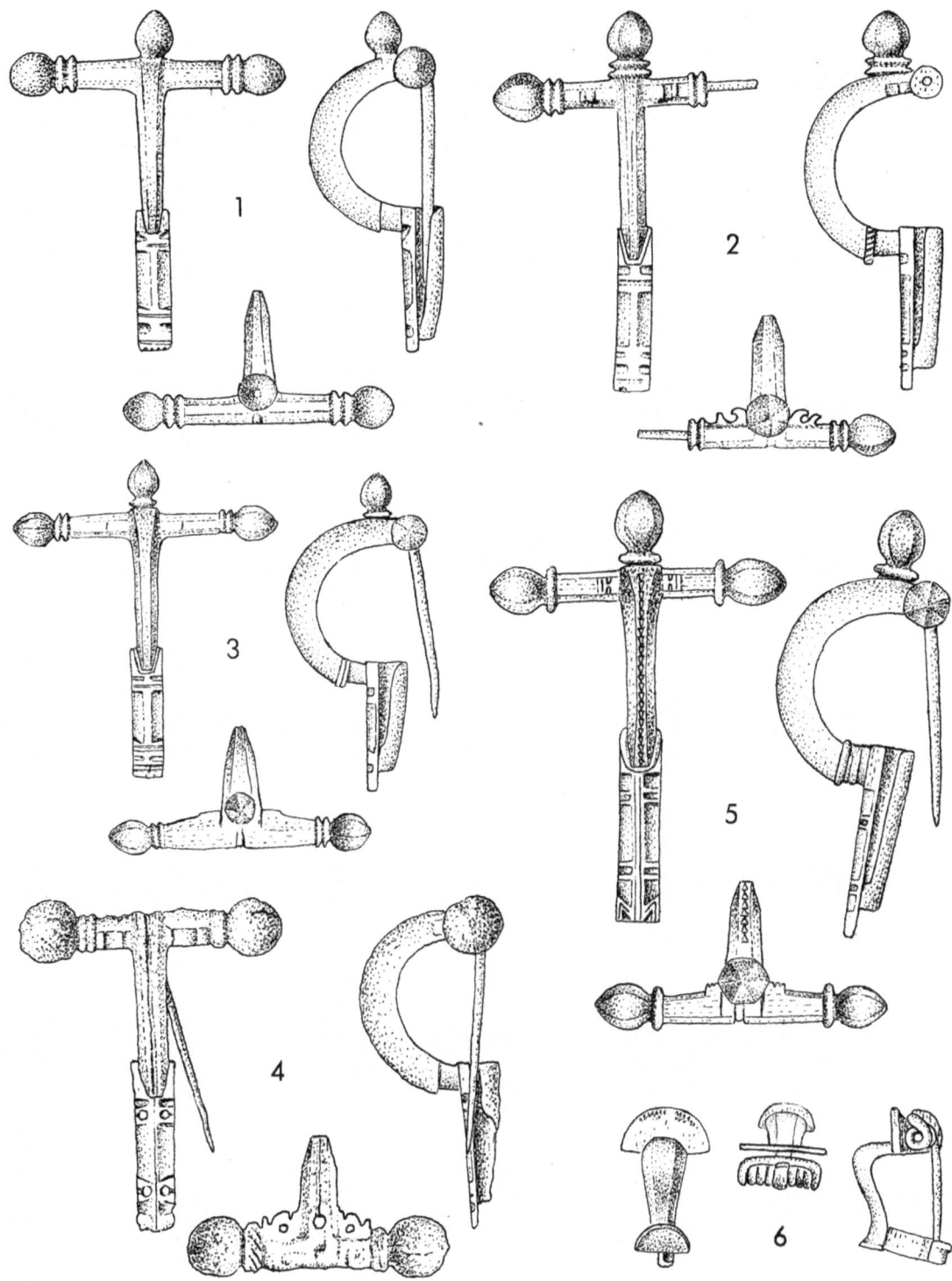

Fig. 82. Fibulae from the skeleton graves: 1-grave 9; 2-grave 10;
3-grave 32; 4-grave 29; 5-grave 25; 6-grave 35.
Scale 1:2

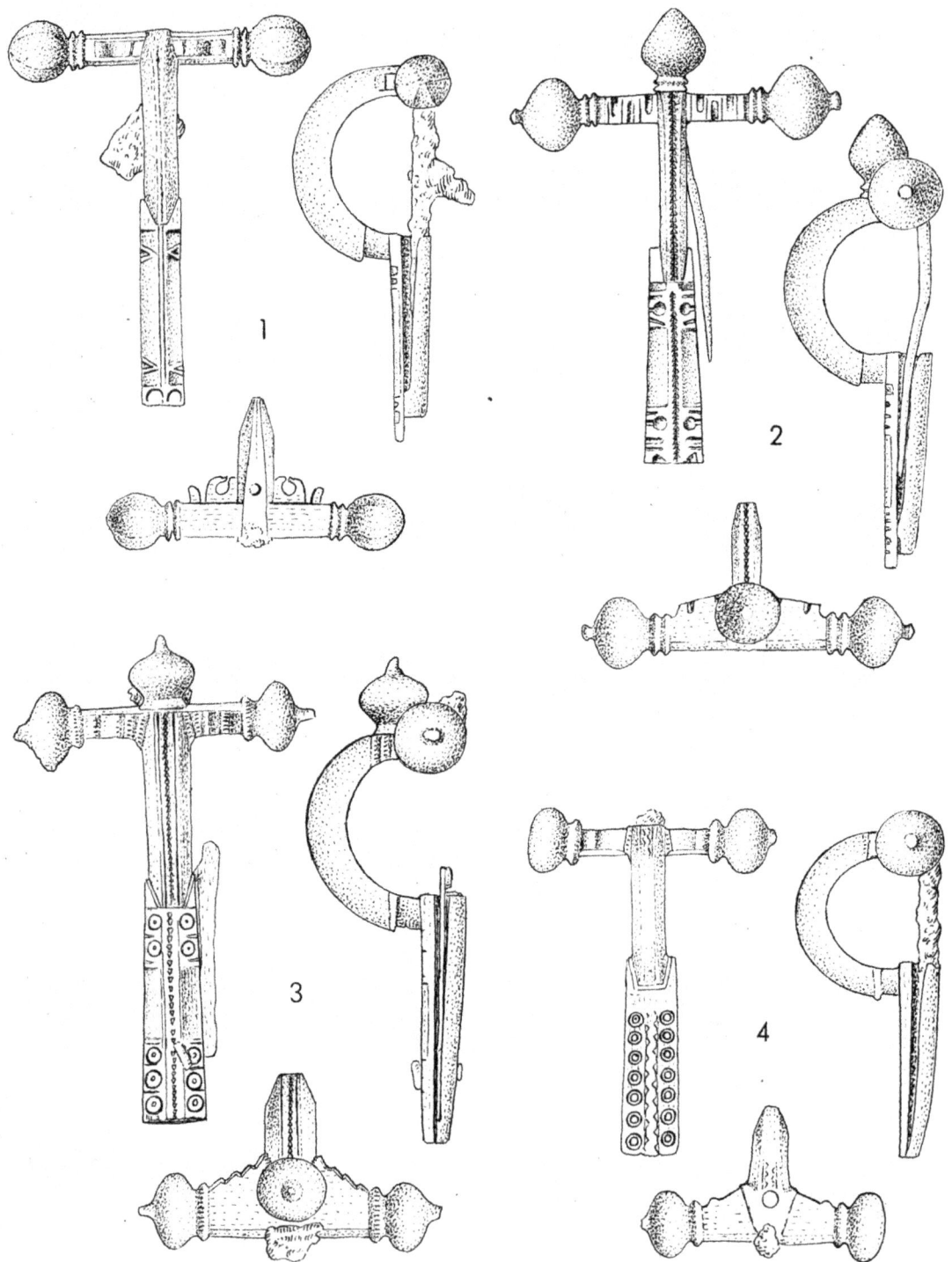

Fig. 83.   Fibulae from the skeleton graves: 1-grave 84;   2-grave 7;
3-grave 12;   4-grave 15.   Scale 1:2

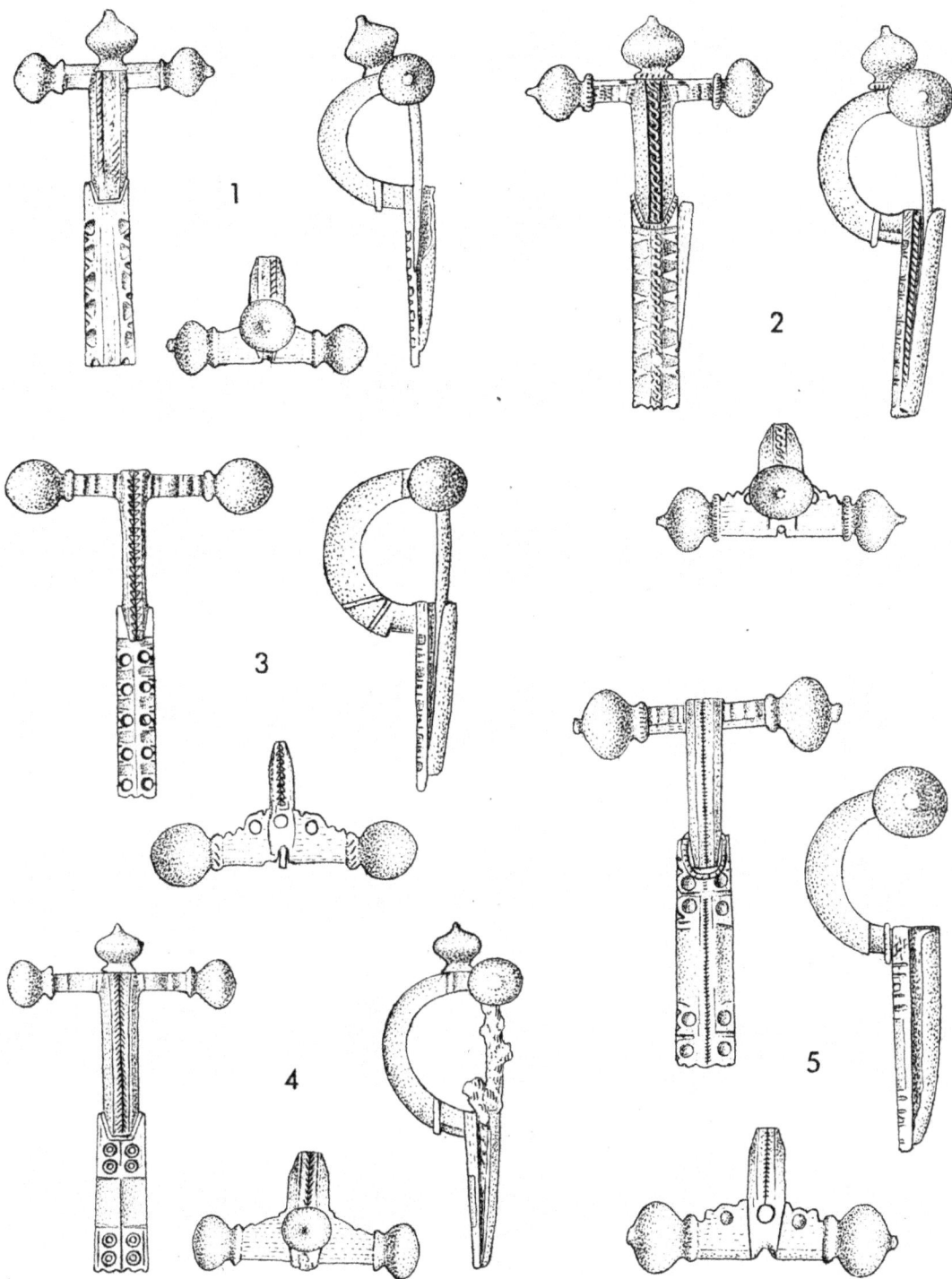

Fig. 84.   Fibulae from the skeleton graves: 1-grave 20; 2-grave 103;
3-grave 144; 4-grave 167; 5-damaged grave. Scale 1:2

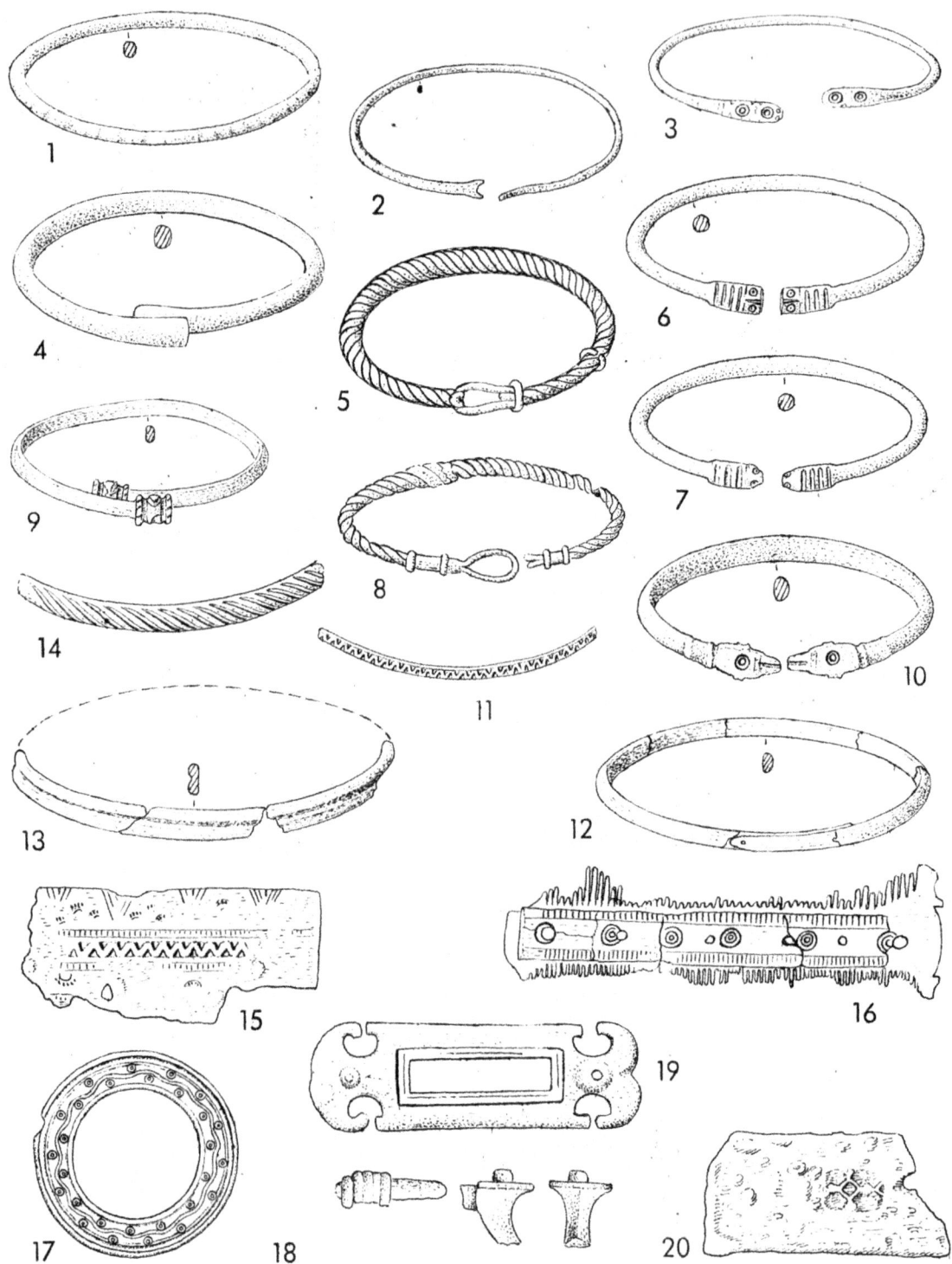

Fig. 85. Ornaments from the skeleton graves: 1-grave 3; 2,5,10-grave 41;
3,12-grave 36; 4,14-grave 2; 6,7-grave 14; 8-grave 52;
9-grave 55; 11,17-grave 1; 13-grave 21; 15,16-grave 6.
Finds from the cremation graves: 18-grave 96; 19-grave 69;
20-grave 121. Scale 1:2

Plate I.   1,2-grave 2;   3,4-grave 5;   5-grave 7;   6-grave 9

Plate II.   1-grave 12;   2-grave 15;   3-grave 18;   4-graves 19, 20;   5-grave 25
             6-graves 29, 30

Plate III.   1-grave 36;   2-grave 70;   3-graves 82, 83;   4-grave 65;   5-grave
             74   6-grave 92

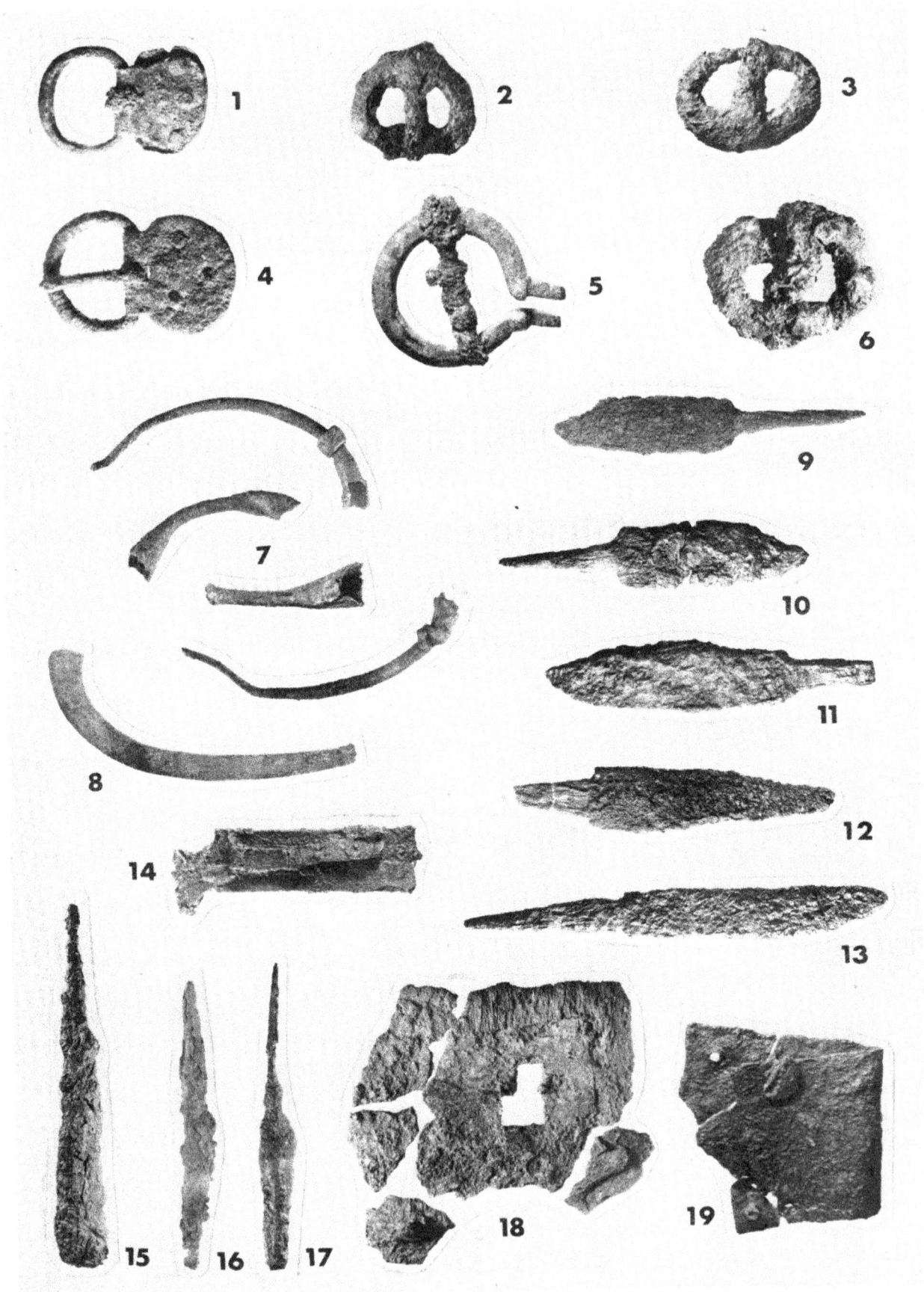

Plate IV. Metal Objects. 1-grave 30; 2,15-grave 144; 3-grave 46; 4,13-
grave 32; 5,10-grave 31; 6-grave 18; 7-grave 92; 8-grave 96;
9,16-grave 103; 11-grave 25; 12-grave 40; 14-grave 105; 17-
grave 48; 18-grave 73; 19-grave 95

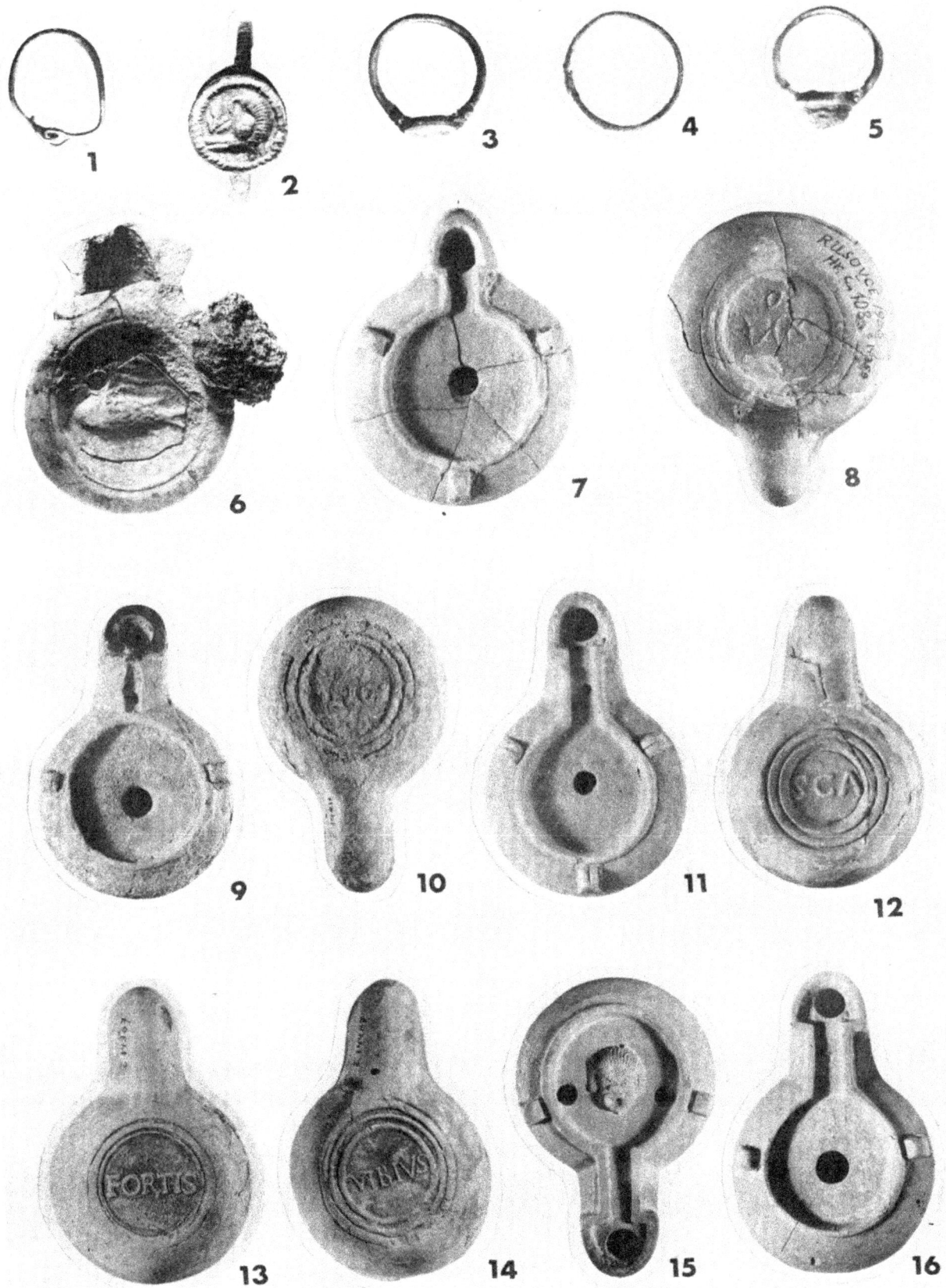

Plate V.   Finger Rings; Lamps: 1-grave 21; 2-grave 12; 3-grave 41;
4-grave 53; 5-grave 144; 6-grave 104; 7,8-grave 108; 9,10-
grave 66; 11,12-grave 97; 13-grave 110; 14-grave 121; 15-
grave 115; 16-grave 156

Plate VI. Miscellaneous: 1-grave 1; 2-grave 167; 3,6-grave 18; 4-grave 21;
5-grave 11; 7-grave 29; 8,9-strayfinds; 10-grave 78; 11-grave 36

www.ingramcontent.com/pod-product-compliance
Lightning Source LLC
Chambersburg PA
CBHW061300270326
41932CB00029B/3416

9 780904 531428